What People Are Sa

"Albert Einstein once said, 'We can't solve problems by using the same kind of thinking we used when we created them.' Judy Carman's superb book promotes the thinking that is necessary to respond to today's critical problems. She advocates a paradigm shift from a world of violence, oppression, injustice, domination, misogyny, aggression, carnism, and patriarchy, to one of love, compassion, cooperation, partnership, sharing, caring, justice, veganism and other positive values. At a time when climate experts are increasingly warning that we may have only a few years to make unprecedented changes in order to have a chance to avert a climate catastrophe and climate events are becoming more frequent and severe, it is urgent that Judy Carman's cogent message be widely shared and heeded. *Homo Ahimsa* has the potential to have the kind of transformative impact that Rachel Carson's *Silent Spring* and Frances Moore Lappe's *Diet For a Small Planet* had. I very strongly recommend it."

– **Richard H. Schwartz, Ph.D.**, author of *Judaism and Vegetarianism, Judaism and Global Survival, Who Stole My Religion? Revitalizing Judaism and Applying Jewish Values to Help Heal our Imperiled Planet,* and *Mathematics and Global Survival,* President Emeritus of Jewish Veg

"Many thinking people today recognize that our old species, Homo Sapiens, stands at a crossroads. One fork turns toward extinction and the other toward an enlightened collaboration among all forms of life to save the planet and one another. Judy Carman's latest book, *Homo Ahimsa,* is a guide toward the road affirming life; it extends the holy messages of different traditions with the force and enlightenment of a New New Testament, of a deeply informed New Scripture: it is that important! It is must reading for anyone interested in human enlightenment and survival."

– **Lee Slonimsky,** Poet and Manager of the Animal Rights hedge fund Green Hills Partners

"Judy Carman skillfully addresses the main problem facing our world today, and inspires readers to go deeper in understanding, and more effectively contribute to a positive future."
– **Madeleine Tuttle**, Swiss visionary artist

"Judy Carman's insight has done the heavy lifting of assembling a profound realization of who we are. In devotion to a higher love, she puts us on her shoulders, so we may see a sacredness of life hidden by illusion…and wake-up to a reality of loving kindness. *Homo Ahimsa* is gifted food for the soul."
– **Frank Lane**, serial CEO, inventor, author of *Be In Heaven Now* and *Plant Powered Enlightenment.*

"In her book *Look a Lion in the Eye*, author and UN worker Kathryn Hulme, on a 1971 camera safari in Africa, reflected on the wild creatures' long, slow stares at her, and realized that "The animals are waiting for us to move up so they can follow. . . ." that is, up Jacob's ladder of spiritual evolution. Judy Carman, in Homo Ahimsa, shows us that we cannot wait for the working out of the laws of spiritual evolution that Hulme mentioned. It is urgent that destructive and predatory Homo "Sapiens" be transformed into nonviolent Homo Ahimsa within a decade, by watering the seeds of mutual respect and love that already exist in each of us. The survival of life on Earth depends on it. In Section One Ms. Carman provides abundant information that shows *why* it must occur so soon; in Section Two she offers us *how* actions we can take, both individually and in groups, can bring about a beautiful and renewed earth in which all inhabitants live together in peace…This book is a lifeline."
– **Gracia Fay Ellwood**, Editor of "The Peaceable Table," and author of *Taking the Adventure: Faith and our Kinship with Animals*

"Judy Carman's book explains some important truths… Meditation, observing a vegan diet, observing ahimsa in our relationships with others and with the economy, and even ahimsa towards ourselves, is the basis of all authentic spirituality."
– **Keith Akers**, author of *The Lost Religion of Jesus: Simple Living and Nonviolence in Early Christianity* and *Disciples: How Jewish Christianity Shaped Jesus and Shattered the Church.*

"Carman presents the current situation well, yet doesn't leave us feeling hopeless. She provides actions as an antidote to despair, and I appreciate the good news she includes. Hopeful and optimistic."
– **Dianne Waltner**, founder Wichita Animal Rights Group

I am deeply grateful to have read *Homo Ahimsa*. Even though we humans are causing immense suffering and violence on Earth, Judy's book inspires us to foresee a positive future; that as a species, we can actually achieve world peace and live in harmony with all life. The horrors we inflict on other sentient beings, to the environment, and other human beings bring me to tears. Still, it also gives me hope and a reason for living, that humanity can indeed awaken to our natural compassion. It also propels me to do more to share nonviolent veganism with many more people. *Homo Ahimsa* is truly The Book About *Who We Really Are and How We're Going to Save the World*. Excellent, highly recommended.
– **Michael Lanfield**, Author of *The Lost Love; Return to the Gentle Sea: For the Love That Lives in Everyone; Creating a Beautiful World,* and vegan advocate; Weareinterconnected.com

"Carman's luminous book opened my heart again to believe that, given the extreme moment in which we find ourselves, humans' path to becoming Homo Ahimsa could actually happen. The COVID-19 pandemic, along with climate change, provides that opportunity, as both can so clearly be tied to animal exploitation."
– **Kate Lawrence**, author of *The Practical Peacemaker* and Denver Vegans Organizer

HOMO AHIMSA*

* *Ahimsa is a Sanskrit word meaning "non-harm." Mahatma Gandhi took a vow of ahimsa and embraced its broader meaning of nonviolence and compassion for all people and all earthlings. His nonviolent resistance, based on ahimsa values and "truth force," inspired the world.*

HOMO AHIMSA

Who We *Really* Are

And How We're Going
To Save The World

Judy McCoy Carman, M.A.

Homo Ahimsa: Who We Really Are and How We're Going to Save the World

Copyright by Judy McCoy Carman, M.A., 2020
Print Edition
Circle of Compassion Publishing, 2020
Lawrence, KS
Peacetoallbeings.com

Printed in the United States of America
ISBN: 978-0-578-70301-5

Dedication

To Michael and to my precious children and grandchildren who bring me endless joy. May the joy you have given me return to you infinitely.

In loving memory of my parents and my dear daughter, Judy.

To all the movers and shakers out there, of all species, bringing in the new era of love, peace and Homo Ahimsa.

And to joy, healing and liberation for all beings.

CONTENTS

FOREWORD

By Dr. Will Tuttle, Ph.D.

With every passing day, we are seeing the consequences of our routine and relentless mistreatment of animals escalate. Disease and pandemics proliferate, ecosystems deteriorate, and equality and human rights fade while we seem powerless to reverse these trends. At the same time, we are learning more about the beneficial effects of whole, organic vegetables, fruits, and grains on our physical health, and we are reawakening the ancient wisdom teaching of the Golden Rule and its relevance for our treatment not just of each other, but of the animals with whom we share this Earth.

There are silver linings in our current situation. Questioning the narratives of our herding culture, we can each contribute to the evolutionary imperative called for in these pages. The key to awakening from the violence of Homo Sapiens to the harmony of Homo Ahimsa is in this questioning, and in our efforts to embody the eternal truth of the interconnectedness of all expressions of life. This is our generational calling: to understand our true nature so that we can live more healthy and productive lives, and contribute to the harmonious world that is a natural reflection of awakened awareness.

Personally, I am grateful to the wisdom teachings I discovered many years ago that came not just from the Christian tradition I was raised in, but particularly from the ancient Asian Buddhist and Taoist traditions. Besides advocating simplicity, kindness, humility, and harmonizing ourselves with the larger world of nature, they taught me the importance of eating a plant-based diet. As a vegan of forty years now, I feel my life and my destiny have been improved immeasurably by these ancient teachings advocating mindful living.

Physical health, psychological health, spiritual health, cultural health, and ecological health are all interconnected. When we pay for and eat foods from animals, we act in disconnected and heartless ways not only toward the animals, but also toward the people who have to do the terrible work of killing animals all day, and to those who go hungry because we are feeding valuable grain to pigs, chickens, cows, and farmed fish so that we can eat meat, eggs, fish, and dairy products. These poor animals are inefficient converters of grain into animal protein, saturated fat, and cholesterol, and create terrible pollution problems that lead to environmental devastation and species extinction as we cut down forests, overfish the oceans, and pollute and waste water in order to grow feedstock. And then, to compound these problems, eating meat and dairy products is the driving force behind the many diseases that cause us misery, such as heart disease, diabetes, osteoporosis, arthritis, kidney disease, obesity, infectious pandemics, and many forms of cancer.

By hardening our hearts to the suffering of the birds, mammals, fish, and other people we harm for food, we also harden our arteries and cut our lives short. As this book demonstrates so well, being kind to others benefits not only them but ourselves as well. This is the wisdom awakening in us that this book celebrates and toward which it calls. Each of us can not only savor and contemplate our next iteration, Homo Ahimsa, but also do the inner and outer work to help make this a reality in our world. This is the beckoning doorway toward which our more evolved future selves invite us.

There is no greater gift we can give the world than our effort to understand and practice the nonharmfulness of ahimsa that shines in our hearts as our true nature. The essential challenge we face is to apprehend the wisdom that underlies this book. Although it has ancient roots, we are called to rediscover it today because institutions and interests that profit from disease, devastation, and oppression are suppressing it.

Each one of us can stop being part of the problem, and become part of the solution! Thank you for reading, contemplating, and endeavoring to embody the awareness conveyed in these pages. You can help yourself and all of us. We are all interrelated.

❖ Dr. Will Tuttle is the award-winning visionary author of the international best-seller, *The World Peace Diet: Eating for Spiritual Health and Social Harmony*. He presents globally and is featured in many documentaries and online broadcasts. Learn more about Dr. Tuttle at Worldpeacediet.com.

ACKNOWLEDGMENTS

Acknowledgments are difficult to write, because we don't want to leave anyone out. When you really think about it, everything we finish (like this book) is a result of the influence of everyone who has ever impacted our lives, whether in a positive or a painful way. My dream is that this book will play some small part in bringing about a culture of love, liberation and peace for my grandchildren who now, in their young lives, live in a violent and troubled world. So I thank them for motivating me to get these words on paper. And I dream, as Jesus lights my way, of a world of kindness, nonviolence and freedom for all our animal cousins, who inspire me daily with the lessons they teach and the invitation they repeatedly extend us to enter into the sacred interconnectedness of all life. My heart is full of gratitude for all the activists who have gone before us and those now living, who refuse to give up on the vision that we human beings can stop our violent ways, heal the damage we've done, and create a world of peace for all earthlings.

I am grateful beyond words to the amazing activists who helped directly with this book: Keith Akers, Michael Carman, Gracia Fay Ellwood, JoAnn and Sarina Farb, Thomas Jackson, Frank Lane, Michael Lanfield, Kate Lawrence, Lisa Levinson, Anna McCoy, Victoria Moran, Shannon Murphy, Holly Neber, Sailesh Rao, Reverend Carol Saunders, Richard Schwartz, Lee Slonimsky, Veda Stram, Will and Madeleine Tuttle, Dianne Waltner and Ann Wilson. Great inspiration also came from the creek, trees, flowers, grasses, cows, turkeys, frogs, and birds around Ahimsa Acres, where I live, who kept singing all this to me. In a way, it was they who wrote the book, for truly it is a plea from all of them to us.

PREFACE

Homo Sapiens has ravaged the earth for thousands of years. Warnings of species extinction and ecosystem collapse have been getting louder by the day. But while we may tremble to see the damage our species has done, we may be heading, at the same time, toward a paradigm shift in human consciousness that can bring us and all earthlings out of these dark times and into a new way of living. If you have opened this book, it is likely that you are here now to take part in this shift, to help midwife the birth of a liberated world, to ascend to higher consciousness, and to do your part to heal the wounds humanity has caused in the world. Thank you.

I have kids and grandkids, like many of you, and like the other animals of the world. They are so precious to me that I can barely think of them without my heart filling with joy and my eyes filling with tears, just knowing they are in my life. And yet, I see all around them so many troubles. Like you, I long to do everything I can, in my own small way, to undo the damage human beings have done to the air and water, to nature, and to all the beings who share this home with us. And while the situation is drastic, I believe with all my heart that it is not too late to turn this around. I believe there is still time to create a planetary home of love, nonviolence, kindness, and celebration for all the children of Earth, and I believe that we can become *Homo Ahimsa. Ahimsa* is the Sanskrit word for non-harm. Its broader meaning includes nonviolence, lovingkindness, compassion, reverence and love for all living beings.

This book is for everyone who longs for a world in which there are no more wars or violent crimes, no more hate and prejudice, no more poisonous pollution. That revolutionary world is possible, and we can make it happen. This is not an impossible dream. We can stop the mindless destruction and domination of people, animals, and nature. If you doubt that we can reach the higher consciousness and healing that is now required of us, please stay with me. May your faith be renewed in humanity. May you believe with me that we can do this.

Within the pages of this book you will find:

- Why human beings must wake up spiritually to our true nature as Homo Ahimsa in order to heal the damage we've done;
- Why vegan ethics and ahimsa spirituality are the primary keys to stopping the sixth extinction, world-wide pollution, desertification, world hunger, rain forest destruction, and the slaughter of billions of land and marine animals;
- Why partnership, non-anthropocentric living is essential to liberating both animals and people from the reign of patriarchy and the dominator mindset that has lasted for thousands of years;
- Why we cannot wait for corrupt governments and corporations to fix this: it is up to us, but we can do it;
- How our spiritual nature can empower us to deal with anger, grief, and compassion fatigue so that we do not give up;
- How to keep the faith that we have a chance at this; we can bring Mother Earth and all earthlings back from the brink.
- Why animal rights can no longer be considered a fringe movement: without a massive switch to plant-based eating, an end to animal agriculture, and reverence for all life, the current race to annihilation will rage on.

Why I am Writing to You: It's because you and I are hearing a calling from our spirits to take action. We want to help bring an end to the violence and destruction that faces us now. We are hearing the shrill warnings of catastrophe every day as more scientific results roll in. But take heart. There is a lot that each one of us can do to turn this around. We can, and we will.

Many activists have dedicated their lives to saving nature, animals, and people from the devastation caused by human greed and lust for power. And while there have been victories, such as the end of legalized slavery and stoning of women in some countries, and some protections for a few endangered species, nevertheless, many entities with corporate, political and religious power have continued the seemingly unstoppable destruction of trees, water, air, people, animals, and nature. Our activism has not been enough to stop this annihilation. We are at a critical moment in time. Let's look at this from the highest vantage point.

It is from this perspective that we discover the good news—great news, in fact. There is a holistic—body, mind, spirit—revolution going on at the same time these tragedies are unfolding. On the one hand, the demand for endless wealth, growth and domination forges ahead, leaving nature polluted and billions of animals and people dead. But on the other hand, a higher consciousness of compassion, equality, mutual respect, and partnership is rising in response. We are leaving behind the dominator model of living, because it leads only to destruction. And we are learning how to transform ourselves and create a world that works with the partnership model. Millions of super heroes are on their way, and you are one of them.

Super Heroes in Action: PJ McKosky arrived at BeeBee Farms with friends on New Year's Eve to rescue chickens who had been abandoned while the farm was going bankrupt, running out of feed, and unable to pay for propane to heat the barns. This so-called "natural" and "pasture-raised" chicken farm was a hellish mess of dead and dying chickens confined in barns filled with lung-searing ammonia and feces. While farm workers cut off heads without mercy, PJ and the other rescuers saved as many as they could. PJ writes, "I kept thinking of the saying, 'Whoever saves a single life is considered to have saved the whole world,' as I picked up each broken bird. Each bird we saved was a victory of sorts, and that reality grounded me in not succumbing to feelings of impotence and anger."[1]

It is this spirit of unconditional and selfless love that is transforming our species and demonstrating how to live as Homo Ahimsa. PJ and millions of other human beings are proving that we do not have to live in bondage anymore to the violent worldview of domination. We can free everyone and create an ahimsa-based world of partnership, freedom, love, and compassion for *and with* all who live here.

The New Humanity Coming into Form: In my book, *Peace to All Beings: Veggie Soup for the Chicken's Soul,* I wrote that we can become Homo Ahimsa. This emerging Homo Ahimsa does the least harm and the most good, feels compassion and unconditional love for all beings, and lives a nonviolent life. Many futurists are declaring that our species is undergoing a "Global Mind Change," a "Great Awakening," a great paradigm shift into the higher consciousness of the Divine Feminine and leaving behind the dominator world view of the patriarchy under which Homo Sapiens and all life has labored for so long.[2]

> *The present chaos is not the end of the world,*
> *but the labor pains of a new earth and*
> *a new humanity coming into form.*
> Pierre Teilhard de Chardin

Homo Ahimsa *is* the "new humanity coming into form." Ahimsa is the vow that Gandhi took to declare that he was dedicated to nonviolence and lovingkindness, not just to other human beings, but to all creatures. Nearly all religions have, within their core teachings, the Golden Rule—Do unto others as you would have them do unto you. It is considered humanity's highest calling. Why would these religions imagine such an ideal if it were not possible for Homo Sapiens to transform from a clever but destructive creature, into Homo Ahimsa—human beings whose actions are aligned with the Golden Rule?

A Spiritual, Transformational Movement: This is, at its deepest roots, a spiritual movement. Many people have rejected or lost interest in formal religion because it has been complicit in much of the devastation we face today. But spirituality transcends organized religion. It is a metaphysical and mysterious impulse that visits us and moves us to say "no" to the status quo that is causing so much suffering, pain, and violence. Some may call this impulse a nudging from God or Jesus or Krishna or, perhaps, their higher selves. Whatever we choose to call the Source of this Divine Intelligence, it is what brings people to dedicate their lives to causes beyond themselves.

Many social movements, including those inspired by Gandhi and Martin Luther King, Jr., got much of their selfless determination from their faith. They believed that what they were doing was aligned with the abiding Love that dwells in the very air we breathe.

We are witnessing a massive spiritual awakening. Why do we say "spiritual?" Isn't the mess we're in understandable by simple logic? The facts are in our face—we are in desperate times, caused by our own actions and inactions. But no, logic is not enough. Logic alone will not get us there; that is obvious. There is overwhelming data to show us every day what new reef has died; how many whales have beached and died from sonar testing, fish nets and ingesting plastic; how many acres of rainforest have been cut down for the cattle industry. The facts are there. Our egos, our logical minds know. But it is in our hearts and souls that the passion and love to stop the violence resides.

We know now that the best healing for an individual is holistic. It needs to address the physical, mental and spiritual life of the suffering one. Without the body, mind, and spirit being nourished and cared for, the healing will not be complete. This is just as true for the healing of the world which we must undertake as a species. When we engage in healing at the level of spirit, we enter the mystical realm. There we find ourselves nurtured and strengthened by the Divine Love that animates and breathes life into all beings. Passion and faith begin to do their work in us so that we enter into partnership with the Divine and with all life and discover what is ours to do in this transformative work.

The Animal Rights Movement of Nonviolence and Love is No Longer on the Fringe. It is a Primary Key to the Survival of Humanity and Life on Earth. The ongoing and determined movement for the liberation of animals has taken on a new and rich significance now for all humanity. Those who have recoiled at the very idea of eating something labeled "vegan," will soon be unable to deny that the answers to our very survival as a species, and that of millions of other species, are intrinsically embedded in the paradigm of lovingkindness and non-harm. Animal rights and veganism stare patriarchy in the face and declare: living as dominators and exploiters of others is *not working*. And because of its dark and violent nature, such domination is imploding in upon itself, causing chaos, and leading us all toward annihilation.

"As the left hardens its commitment to fighting climate change, social injustice, and rampant capitalism, the question of what to do about animals will become inescapable...," writes Emily Atkins. The many crucial issues of healing the wounds of Mother Earth, caring for those people who are marginalized, and bringing peace to the world, can no longer be seen as separate from the rights of animals to also be healed and liberated. All these issues intersect, and these desperate times are bringing that into clear focus. There is no way to heal the damage Homo Sapiens has done without ending the exploitation and violence against animals; no way to have peace on earth as long as we continue the brutal war against animals; no way to have equality for women as long as we brutalize, rape and kill female animals. Atkins points out that, to the extent that we rid our earth of animal agriculture, "...waterways would flush out pollution; aquifers would replenish. Billions of lives would be saved, human lives very much among them. Or, you know," she quips, "we could keep eating hamburgers."[3]

> *Until we have the courage to recognize cruelty for*
> *what it is—whether its victim is human or animal—*
> *we cannot expect things to be much better in this world...*
> *We cannot have peace among men whose hearts*
> *delight in killing any living creature. By every act*
> *that glorifies or even tolerates such moronic delight*
> *in killing we set back the progress of humanity.*
> Rachel Carson

Will Kymlicka explains that, "Social justice movements can't be too cavalier in dismissing the animal rights movement, because in doing so, they're arguing that humans are inherently a superior species and thus have moral dominion over the earth. That mindset actually harms the fight for racial, gender, and other social equalities." Kymlicka notes that ten studies have shown that the belief that there is a hierarchy among species is directly associated with dehumanization of various groups of human beings. "It [belief in the hierarchy of species] exacerbates racism, sexism, homophobia, and reduces support for fair wages for workers..."[4]

The foundation of this book you are holding in your hands is built upon the uplifting certainty and radical faith that we can accomplish this epic transformation of our species. But we may not have much time. We will look at how to make this transition in upcoming chapters. We will explore specific steps that every person can take to heal the world, and practices to strengthen us for our own transformation and the work ahead.

Before we forge ahead into the following chapters, let us pause for a few moments in silence and listen: hear the earth calling; hear the animals crying; feel your own soul and Divine Intelligence guiding you. Take some time and listen.

No peace lies in the future which is not
hidden in this present little instant.
Fra Giovanni Giocondo, 1513

PART ONE: WHY

Why We Must Rise Above Homo Sapiens
and Transcend to Our Higher Nature
and Our Spiritual Destiny Now

CHAPTER ONE

Homo Sapiens Has Brought
Us All to the Brink

I'm traveling around the world now...
trying to tell people what's happening in the world,
the mess that we've made and the fact that unless we
all get together to help the environment we all share,
then it may be too late. The window of time is closing.
And it's not enough just to wave placards and say,
"Climate change!" The point is to take actual
action. To do your bit.
Jane Goodall[1]

A few current indicators show just how close to the brink we may be.

- **Climate Healers'** Sailesh Rao warns that due to our reckless treatment of the Earth and the devastation caused by animal agriculture, "If we continue with business as usual, we will likely kill off virtually 100% of all wild animals by 2026..." His research survey reveals that over half of all animals of the wilderness have been killed since 1970. He predicts that if we do not create a vegan world and eliminate animal agriculture, massive chaos will be the result for millions of people who will be refugees when land becomes uninhabitable. Dr. Rao considers animal agriculture the leading cause of "deforestation, habitat destruction, wildlife extinction, ocean dead zones, soil degradation and climate change, because it is resource intensive and highly inefficient. Animals eat almost 40 times what they produce as meat, dairy or eggs. 83% of agricultural land is currently used for raising farm animals for food."[2]

In his White Paper, Dr. Rao concludes, "The necessary global transition to a plant-based economy can be achieved through concerted, grassroots action..."[3]

- **The Living Planet Index** estimates that sixty percent of wild vertebrates died off in forty years. "...[W]e have known for many years that we are driving the planet to the brink," the authors declare.[4]

- **The Intergovernmental Platform On Biodiversity Ecosystem Services (IPBES)** warns that "The lack of active and productive ecosystems will cause many severe challenges in the next 10-15 years. How soon and how effectively we deal with these challenges will determine the fate of our civilization."[5]

- **The Proceedings of the National Academy of Sciences (PNAS)**, in a 2017 study on biological annihilation revealed that the sixth mass extinction, within which we are now living, is worse than previously thought. They state, "The massive loss of populations [of wildlife] is already damaging the services ecosystems provide to civilization." They point to multiple causes including destruction of habitats, pollution, human population growth and overconsumption. All of these, they say, "trace to the fiction that perpetual growth can occur on a finite planet..." They warn "that the sixth mass extinction is already here and the window for effective action is very short, probably two or three decades at most. All signs point to ever more powerful assaults on biodiversity in the next two decades, painting a dismal picture of the future of life, including human life."[6]

The PNAS further reports in "The Biomass Distribution on Earth" that our population of 7.6 billion people makes up a mere .01% of all living organisms, but we have destroyed 83% of all wild mammals and 50% of all plants. When looking at the total biomass of all mammals, the remaining wild animals make up 4%, human beings make up 36%. Farmed animals, raised for their flesh, milk and eggs, make up the remaining 60%, even though before the agricultural age began 10,000 years ago, those animals (as they are bred today) did not even exist.[7]

- **The United Nations**. "The Week," a popular mainstream magazine, reports on the U.N. prediction that we have about ten years to "avoid the worst outcomes." Climate Chief Patricia Espinosa, does not hold back when she declares, "If we continue to produce, consume, to function as we are doing now … we know that we are going toward a catastrophe."[8]

- **The International Union for the Conservation of Nature's Biodiversity Conservation Group**'s Director, Jane Smart, declared that, "Nature is declining at rates unprecedented in human history." Her organization's 2019 "planetary health check" concluded that "human civilization was in jeopardy from the accelerating decline of the Earth's natural life-support systems."[9]

- **The Unifying Fields Foundation's** "Beyond Climate Change: An integral solution" found that "about 45% of the world's forests and ecosystems have either been removed or are seriously degraded. Animal farming and unsustainable land-use are the main reason for this massive reduction in the earth's vital and precious assets… In 2017 about 70% of all agricultural land was used for grazing animals. Of the remainder of the land, 40% was used to grow crops for animals. Thus only 18% of agricultural land is used to grow [plant] food for people."[10]

- **The Worldwatch Institute** warned as early as 2004: "Yet, as environmental science has advanced, it has become apparent that the human appetite for animal flesh is a driving force behind virtually every major category of environmental damage now threatening the human future— deforestation, erosion, fresh water scarcity, air and water pollution, climate change, biodiversity loss, social injustice, the destabilization of communities and the spread of disease."[11]

- **Science Magazine**'s 2018 metanalysis study of 38,700 farms in 119 countries, by authors Poore and Nemecek, found that, of the world's arable land, 83% is used by animal agriculture, including dairy and eggs. The authors worry that "widespread behavioral change will be hard to achieve in the narrow timeframe remaining to… prevent further, irreversible biodiversity loss."[12]

- **Faunalytics** tells us that a staggering seventy billion cows, pigs, sheep, goats and chickens are slaughtered each year around the world.[13] What about fishes and others who live in the now-polluted waters? According to **A Well-Fed World**, fisheries "kill hundreds of billions of aquatic animals every year, far more than any other industry. In the past 50 years, 90% of large fish populations have been exterminated." Fish who are raised in captivity make up about thirty percent of aquatic animals consumed. Forty percent of those individuals die from disease and crowding before being slaughtered.[14] These numbers do not count all the aquatic animals who are killed in nets and thrown away as trash. Nor do they count the number of animals killed for experiments, leather, down, fur, and entertainment (such as horse and dog races, circuses, zoos, etc.). Not counted in these figures as well are those killed by hunters, trappers, and ranchers and the billions of male chicks ground up alive because they are useless to the egg industry. The numbers are so overwhelming, our minds cannot really comprehend them. The level of violence toward innocent animals and the immeasurable suffering that they endure has reached a tipping point. We simply cannot continue to cause this massive misery and expect to create the world of peace of which we dream.

• **Sea Shepherd**'s Paul Watson tells us that the oceans are the life support system of the earth. Phytoplankton live in the ocean and produce fifty percent of the oxygen that all life depends on. But since 1950 their populations have plummeted by forty percent. As Captain Watson warns, "If phytoplankton were to disappear tomorrow we would all die."[15]

• **Pandemics.** Just as this book was about to go to press, Covid-19 and the corruption and confusion associated with it disrupted the lives of nearly every person on earth. This virus, along with nearly all the other pandemics, has its origin in patriarchal control from the top down as well as from the confining and eating of innocent animals. Prior to the ten thousand year reign of animal agriculture, there is evidence that human beings experienced no pandemics at all. This is yet another alarm bell ringing, begging humanity to wake up and see that, if we continue to ravage the Earth and murder animals by the billions, and if we continue to believe the official narrative of those in power, we will lose this luminous chance for planetary awakening.

But what if none of this is true? What if all these publications and statistics are just scare tactics? We all know now that we cannot just blindly believe what we are being told.

Questioning authority and critical thinking are essential if we are to create the world of peace that we want.

What if…?

What if there isn't enough evidence yet? What if these predictions are way off? What if we're not facing annihilation at all? What if, somehow, life support systems for human beings can continue indefinitely despite our relentless, destructive behavior? What if the power elite can "save" us with technology as long as we agree to give up our freedom in order to be "safe?"

Let's suppose for a moment that Homo Sapiens will survive in spite of all that we continue to destroy. If that could be so, here's the big question. **Is it morally and ethically right** to keep killing and drilling and burning and waging war? Is what we are doing kind? Is it loving? Do we dare tell our grandchildren that we supported this destruction with our actions and dollars and did nothing to stop it? Even if all those predictions are way off or totally wrong, our species needs to face up to what we have done to this sacred Earth and all who are trying to live here in spite of us. We need to face the sheer terror we have created here. Whether the predictions are true or not, it is time to discover our true and highest nature as partners, not dominators, of this precious planet that is home to all earthlings, not just us.

Animal liberation is human liberation. Never before has it been so clear that animal liberation, i.e. freeing animals from the tyranny, violence, and domination of human beings, will lead to our own liberation as well. As we watch the animals heading toward annihilation, we realize that we are heading there with them. Somehow, not long ago, it seemed easier to look away from the destruction we were causing, whether actively in our businesses or through our consumerism. But now suddenly animals' rights and liberation are everyone's business, everyone's concern. We simply cannot continue to treat animals and nature so sadistically and expect our own lives and souls to thrive. When we take away the joy of living and life itself from any other being, whether it is directly or indirectly, we lose our own right to joy and life. I don't mean to say that someone can take away our joy, because we harmed another. It happens, not from outside us, but within us, on a soul level.

> *One day the absurdity of the almost universal human*
> *belief in the slavery of other animals will be palpable.*
> *We shall then have discovered our souls and*
> *become worthier of sharing this planet with them.*
> Martin Luther King, Jr.

Nikola Tesla, the inventor of alternating current, among other things, argued that eating animals is immoral. We should make every effort, he pleaded, "to stop the wanton and cruel slaughter of animals, which must be destructive to our morals."

Dr. Will Tuttle explains that our souls are deeply fractured by participating in animal using and killing, because "we are all harmed when any is harmed…"[16]

> *When one tugs at a single thing in nature,*
> *one finds it attached to the rest of the world.*
> John Muir

The patriarchal, dominator worldview has harmed us all. This belief system appears to have erupted with the discovery of animal agriculture and the organized religions, some of which taught that God is male and that only human beings are "made" in "His" image. We, like the animals all around us, have suffered immensely for centuries under the patriarchal belief system that might makes right, that our purpose as human beings is to dominate, exploit, enslave, rape, abuse, and kill those people and animals who can be categorized and objectified as "other." This belief is false, is not based on any facts, but it has allowed those with more aggressive natures to justify their violence toward anyone who gets in their way or who can serve a purpose. And it has permeated the minds of even the gentlest among us and programmed us in ways we are still discovering, as we peel away the layers of lies that hide who we really are. Very few cultures have escaped the influence of this narrative that has been at the root of every human-caused disaster. It has bruised our souls, dulled our empathy, and caused oceans of violence toward all sacred life.

Because of this damaging cultural programming, many people are simply blind to the agony that human beings cause to the animals of the world and to nature, or they believe it is justified because they have been wrongly convinced that it benefits humanity. We can certainly see now that, not only does it not benefit humanity, it is leading to our own destruction. Inner peace and joy that is gained with love limited to human beings is incomplete. A part of the soul remains in chains. As long as we are causing the misery and deaths of the animals we eat and use, our spirits are crying out for liberation.

That is why freeing animals also frees us. We have heard many stories from people who have chosen a vegan life of nonviolence and lovingkindness for all beings. Some began eating plant-based for health reasons and then discovered happily that, as their health improved, they also became more compassionate and open to the suffering and joys of others. Some eliminated animal secretions and flesh from their diets for environmental reasons, to stop pollution and extinction, and they too have found their hearts growing more loving than ever before. Plant-based foods convey a peace of their own to us, and as we cleanse our bodies of the tortured animals and violence we have consumed, the chains of inner violence fall away. In that way, our chances for deep and lasting spiritual joy and transformation become possible, and lead us to our true destiny as Homo Ahimsa.

Slaughterhouse awakening: Several activists and I were downtown one summer night, showing "Earthlings," a film which graphically reveals the way farmed animals are raised and killed. One group of college guys stopped and proceeded to declare that it was all fake. "They don't treat animals like that," they jeered. "PETA just makes that stuff up."

Just as I was about to open my mouth, a big, burly guy who had been standing there watching for a while, began to speak. In a loud, no-nonsense voice, he said to the group of laughing young men, "You're looking at exactly how it is in slaughterhouses. Mostly, it's a lot worse than that." Not to be dissuaded, one of the men challenged him by asking how he could possibly know that. "I worked at the IBP slaughterhouse in Emporia, Kansas, for too many years," he said. "I've seen it all—the most horrible suffering you can ever imagine. And what's really terrible is that the workers get so messed up by the endless violence that they laugh, like you're laughing, at the live cows kicking and mooing as their legs are cut off."

When I asked him how it came about that he stopped working there, he told me that one day, he suddenly realized he wasn't laughing along with the other guys. It was as if something inside him had awakened and he saw the horror of what they all were doing to these innocent, defenseless cows. He was overwhelmed by the dark and heavy energy field of abuse and suffering that permeated the entire place. And that energy field finally got so heavy and powerful that it forced him into a new consciousness. He left the slaughterhouse that day and never returned. He became vegan overnight, and the dark energy began to lift from his mind. Not long after this encounter, I met another man who had worked at the same slaughterhouse. I asked him how it affected him. "The smell of death was everywhere," he said. "I quit after a week. I'd rather starve than eat an animal now."[17]

What else can we call that new awareness but a spiritual awakening? Both men could feel the disconnect between their higher, spiritual feeling of love for animals and their own behavior. In order to find peace in their own hearts, they had to stop the violence and shift to a plant-based way of eating.

Nonviolence is a very high expression of divine love. It is a calling from our spirits, from our hearts. And when we hear that call and live up to our true nature, our power to change the world and free the animals increases dramatically. In other words, vegan living is a spiritual calling and a spiritual path you can count on to lead your heart home and empower you to keep the faith that humanity can transform.

"Operatives" or witnesses for Love? Several years ago, a few days before the Douglas County Fair was to take place, an article in the local Lawrence, Kansas, newspaper warned about the possibility that animal rights "operatives" may come to the Fair to take photos. The Douglas County Fair Board President "said the warnings were a precaution deemed necessary after conversations with officials from county fairs across the state. He said the fair board decided to make participants aware that animal rights operatives may be among them. [He] said such people could attend the fair, take pictures and gather information that could be misconstrued and used in literature lambasting animal cruelty."[18]

Some county fairs have "crying hills" where children, who are forced to give up their 4-H or FFA animal to slaughter, can cry privately. Public tears are frowned upon, and toughness is admired and rewarded. Children, whose tender hearts have opened to the animal they have raised from infancy, are told to close their hearts, deny their natural compassion, and agree with the violent culture that human beings have the right to kill innocent, defenseless young animals for the purpose of receiving money and praise. Whether we were part of 4-H or not, nearly all of us have been programmed in many ways to stifle our empathy and close our hearts to the beings who lie lifeless on our plates.

A sheep named "Fish" calls Animal Place, in Grass Valley, California, home, but he would not be there if the girl who raised and loved him had caved into social and family pressure and sold Fish to slaughter at a California county fair. Luckily the youngster heard about Animal Place, and asked the sanctuary to give Fish a loving home for the rest of his life. It was a blessing that Fish was not being displayed at a "terminal fair." At terminal fairs, no animal can be released to a sanctuary and must, instead, be killed regardless of the tears and heartbreak of the child and the animal he or she raised.[19]

Closing hearts and creating myths to make people look away: In the 1950's, when I was a kid, many giant, odiferous and ugly slaughterhouses were in the central parts of cities. In Kansas City, the stockyards were downtown. My uncles were employed there and were extremely proud of their work. It was not unusual for our family to eat dinner at the Golden Ox restaurant which was situated, believe it or not, right next to the stockyard and its horrific smell. Chicago and other large cities had similarly huge stockyards and slaughterhouses in downtown areas permeating the cities with the unmistakable stench of death. Since then, most of these animal hells have moved out to more rural areas, making the ravaging and torture of billions of land animals less obvious to city dwellers. This paved the way for sensitive children—whose hearts would break if they could see the animals themselves—to buy the myth that they had to eat meat and that the animals were unfeeling machines who did not suffer. The distancing of the killing floors from the cities made it much easier for people to ignore the suffering on their plates. Forget turning the other cheek. Just turn a blind eye, and all will be well.

The extinction of pizza: When the report from IPBES, the Intergovernmental Science-Policy Platform On Biodiversity and

Ecosystem Services, began to go public with news that the future of humanity as a species is at stake, late-night show host Jimmy Kimmel joked that the fear of extinction would not wake people up, but the thought of pizza becoming extinct certainly would.

It's a good joke, but there is some truth in it. Many people do not have the time or energy to spend on such an outlandish notion as our own extinction and that of millions of animal and plant species. Many deny it is happening in order to keep believing that following the status quo will reward them. Many fight it, because their wealth depends on businesses which cannot grow without ripping trees from their roots, killing animals on assembly lines, pouring coal or oil or animal waste or pesticides into streams and rivers and oceans. And many others live in impoverished, polluted or war-torn areas where their immediate survival is at stake, and there is no time or energy for activism. But in every human heart, there dwells the same love that animates all life. Otherwise, they would not be breathing. It is love that penetrates and enlivens us with every breath. If we look into anyone's eyes with humility and care, we can see there the Divine Mystery of Sacred Life Itself looking back at us in wonder.

Nevertheless, it will be difficult for anyone whose livelihood depends on violence to feel the love in their own souls. A Hasidic tale tells the story of a student inquiring of a rabbi why the Torah says to place the sacred words on our hearts instead of in our hearts. The Rebbe answers, "It is because as we are, our hearts are closed, and we cannot place the holy word in our hearts. So we place them on top of our hearts. And there they stay until, one day, the heart breaks and the words fall in."[20]

Hearing the cries, the words "fall in:" Our souls hear the cries of the poisoned prairie dogs, the wolves shot from planes, a mother cow's baby being dragged away, a slaughterhouse worker's rage. We witness the silence that hovers tearfully over a thousand fish lying dead in polluted water and the dead baby seal

14

bludgeoned to death for the fur that no one will buy. Our hearts break from all this. That is why words of love and compassion are falling *into* our hearts. There are enough of us whose hearts have broken open. There are enough of us now, in the nick of time, to bring Homo Ahimsa out of the timid places into the bold, enlivening light. The cries of the animals, all nature, and our own spirits are calling us to bring healing now and reverse the damage we have done.

Millions of you are showing up and demonstrating how to live without bowing down to patriarchy, by creating an entirely new way of living in partnership with all sacred life instead of dominating everything in our path. This is ahimsa living—not only doing the least harm and the most good, but also healing the damage done by us. Evidence is alive everywhere as we will see in Chapter Six.

We are growing as a species from being the destructive domina- tor of all life to being the compassionate and respectful partner of all who share this world with us. We are linked to others in sacred ways we are only beginning to understand. The Genesis chapter of the Bible states that people and animals are *nephesh chaya* or living souls. Unchained from our prison of programmed lies about who we are, we celebrate limitless love, joy and freedom, not just for our species, but for *and with* all. Life makes sense as Homo Ahimsa, because when we live as beings of love and compassion, our actions, thoughts and words are in peaceful alignment with our true nature and highest values. *This is how we pull the world back from the brink.*

Standing in front of the water trucks for the thirsty babies: One soldier in western China must have felt that miraculous alignment one day, if only for a few moments. He was with an army unit that transported strictly rationed water to residents of an arid area. Three kilos (almost a gallon) of water a day were all that was allowed for each person. Farmed animals in this area obviously got very little. As the army unit traveled down the dirt road in their water trucks, a mother cow stepped out onto the road and forced the first truck to stop. She stood there staring at the truck. Drivers cursed at her and tried to scare her with fire. The man, who lived under the illusion that he owned her, whipped her, ripping through her skin.

"The heartrending whines of the old cow sounded so tragic that the soldiers and some of the drivers were moved to tears. At last a soldier said, 'Let me break the rule for once! I'm ready to accept a penalty for this.' He took half a basin of water from the truck (one and a half kilos), and placed it in front of the cow, but to everyone's surprise, the cow did not touch the water."

Instead she called to her baby, and soon her little one came running and drank the water. "With tears in their eyes, the mother cow and her calf licked each other's eyes, silently expressing their love for each other. Then, before anyone had to drive them away, they left on their own."[21]

As this story illustrates, spirit exists, animates us, impels us to action, and lets us know when we are in tune with our true nature as loving, compassionate souls. Most beautiful of all, of course, is the lesson from the mother cow of tender love and willingness to endure pain and suffering in order to care for her child.

This is a tiny microcosm of what we all must now do. We too must stand in front of the water truck, refusing to move, because there are babies for whom we must stand firm and hardened hearts that must break open and tears and love that must fall in.

> *Cruelty to animals is as if man did not love God...there is something so dreadful, so satanic, in tormenting those who have never harmed us, and who cannot defend themselves, who are utterly in our power.*
> Saint John Henry Newman

CHAPTER TWO

Homo Ahimsa Can Heal the Damage We Have Done

Homo Sapiens? In 1758, Carl Linnaeus introduced a name for our human species. Under the influence of deeply entrenched patriarchal and hierarchical programming, he named us "Homo Sapiens," meaning wise man or human. Or, perhaps, he had a sense of humor, as he had certainly seen plenty of evidence of the absence of "wise" in many human affairs by that time. A Merriam-Webster definition of "wise" starts out with lofty terms: "deep understanding, keen discernment, and a capacity for sound judgment." But the iconic dictionary points out that "wise" can also mean "crafty, shrewd, insolent and smart-alecky," along with a synonym, "making light of something usually regarded as serious or sacred." Now that rings a bell.

Calling our species "Sapiens" was a transparently obvious nod to the then-current and wishful worldview that we are the dominator species, "top of the food chain," chosen by God to rule the earth. In fact, however, if we couldn't have figured out how to build safe shelters and develop weapons of destruction, we would have been seriously low on the food chain. So, it's pretty understandable that we looked at our lack of predator tools, such as sharp teeth and claws, not to mention protective fur, and decided we were going to have to get really creative if we were going to survive. But we took predation to a whole new level when we started confining our "prey" in fences, cages, and herds. Our gentle captives—the goats, sheep, and everyone else we decided to use were defenseless against us. No wonder we imagined ourselves to be so powerful.

A modern example of our species' fascination with human power over animals is at the "Scenic View" on Highway I-35, a few miles south of Emporia, Kansas. The scenic view is not a magnificent mountain or glorious canyon. The view is (and I'm not making this up) of the Bazaar Cattle Pens. The proud developers of the signage and the off-ramp to the View hope that you might also see a few cows. Of course, they don't mention the fact that any cows you might see will be brutally slaughtered at a very young age. At the Kansas City Airport, you may see t-shirts for sale with the slogan "I Like Pig Butts. I Cannot Lie." These are attempts by our culture to demean animals to the lowest possible level. For it is only then that we can completely bury the wisdom in our hearts that knows the truth: pigs are our relatives, fully capable of the love the mother cow gave so courageously to her baby; fully capable, indeed, of loving us.

If you want to smile from ear to ear, just do an internet search on "pigs saving children and goats," and your heart will be dancing at the sight of a pig rescuing a drowning boy and another rescuing a goat who is crying for help in the water.

Homo Deus? Yuval Noah Harari, in his book, *Homo Deus: A Brief History of Tomorrow,* proposes the likelihood that we are indeed transforming as a species, but not into Homo Ahimsa. Rather he suggests a darker future. Harari looks at our vast technological capabilities and where they seem to be taking us. He writes as a researcher and reporter of trends, rather than one convinced of the final outcome. He sees signs everywhere of humanity falling more in love with technology without caution. This could lead to a time in the not-too-distant future where computers and biological entities such as ourselves become merged and seen as algorithms to be manipulated at will. Perhaps the wealthy will be paying for "upgrades" to their systems, such as brain implants and bionic parts to replace the ones that are wearing out, as they imagine themselves to be an immortal Homo Deus with endless material happiness, and god-like powers. Deus is Latin for God, of course. Whereas Jesus advised us to serve and love one another, Homo Deus' sight is set on being served at all costs.

Harari notes that these upgraded humans would, no doubt, treat us as we have been treating animals. He warns that we must "...protect humankind and the planet from our own power."[1] The phenomenal economic growth that has taken place in many parts of the world depends entirely on doing everything necessary to continue that growth. "Yet," he suggests, "this same growth destabilizes the ecological equilibrium of the planet..."[2] If we are indeed on the brink of annihilation, and do not turn away from incessant growth, Homo Deus may not have a bionic leg to stand on.

Harari is essentially challenging us to think very carefully about the seductiveness of this world of gadgets and google. "Science," he writes, "is converging on an all-encompassing dogma, which says that organisms are algorithms and life is data processing."[3] Given the current stark reality of massive extinction, pollution, pandemics, desertification, and the other ills of the world, it is likely that if Homo Sapiens does not transform into Homo Ahimsa and instead chooses more Sapiens or the new Deus, then we may be looking at our final chapter, and certainly not a world populated by massive computer networks married to Homo Deus wannabees.

But the good news is that we *can* transform, and many are leading the way, showing us how to do this. There will be more about this in later chapters, but let's remember that when a caterpillar makes a chrysalis, her body actually begins to dissolve into imaginal cells. This has to happen if she is to create an entirely new body and emerge as a glorious creature with wings.

What we see happening in the world today on every front—spiritual, political, economic, personal, psychological—is the disintegration of systems that humans created centuries ago. Patriarchy is disintegrating under the power of the #MeToo movement; the disclosure of sexual predators in the Catholic priesthood; the arrival of women in positions of political, scientific, and corporate leadership; and many other signs of wings unfolding. The patriarchal, hierarchical mindset of domination is being revealed as the impotent, fear-based worldview that it is. Thousands of scientific studies disclose the undeniable facts of animal agriculture's destruction of water, forests, ecosystems, wildlife, farmed animals' lives and families, human health, and air quality. As patriarchy, along with animal agriculture, disintegrates into imaginal cells, Homo Ahimsa is beginning to take on its long-awaited form.

Homo Ahimsa! Sailesh Rao, author of *Carbon Yoga: The Vegan Metamorphosis*, writes, "we can choose to heal the earth or we can choose to kill all life on earth. All lives are at the mercy of our food choices."[4] He uses the analogy of the caterpillar transforming into a butterfly to show us that we can transform from our current life of the hungry caterpillar into the lovely butterfly who sips a bit of nectar and pollinates the plants so that all the damage the hungry caterpillars did to the plants is reversed as new plants take their place. We have been voracious caterpillars too long. We cannot wait another day to begin our transformation to Homo Ahimsa.

But what exactly is Homo Ahimsa? We have seen that Homo Sapiens has not done so well. Homo Deus is definitely no improvement, since it is based on the same cruel, ten thousand year old myth that we have the right to dominate and exploit everything and everyone. Homo Ahimsa can be our new way of living if we choose it. We have claimed, both within our religions and our ethical traditions, that our ideals include mercy; compassion; love for one another; the Golden Rule; nonviolence; world peace; and freedom, healing and abundance for all. We have idealized those qualities, because that is how we want to be. But the deserts, fires, pollution, and animal suffering and death that Homo Sapiens has caused show us how far we have fallen from these ideals. Homo Ahimsa embodies these qualities, not as unreachable ideals, but as a way of living every day.

How has living our true values eluded us for so many centuries? Among other animal species, of course, there is violence. However, one of the most striking aspects of their interactions is restraint. Chimpanzees, for example, can get very upset with each other, according to both researchers of wild and captive chimps. But they have protocols of behavior which prevents interpersonal violence in most cases. The elder woman among them is usually the one who mediates and restores peace for the ones at odds with each other. Observers have reported that she will stand calmly between two arguing males and begin to groom them. The grooming calms them. She grooms one, then the other. When she is sure the drama is over, she calmly leaves the two of them side by side, and they usually, then groom each other.[5] Of course, this makes survival sense for any species to be cooperative with each other, thus cutting down on wounds and other threats to their lives.

Homo Sapiens, with all its high ideals, has been severely handicapped by a harrowing lack of restraint. And, thus, we have threatened, not only our own survival, but that of billions of others. Of course, we *can* continue to destroy, consume, and kill without holding back, but if we do, the devastation will be on us. Homo Ahimsa, like our animal cousins, values restraint. The time for our metamorphosis is now.

Smokey the Bear needed my help. I was about 7 years old when I bumped my head against the wall of "might makes right." I thought I was doing the right thing, but "might" didn't think so. It all started when I saw a poster of Smokey the Bear. He told me that "Only [I] could prevent forest fires." Smokey went viral, 1950's style. I saw him on posters, TV, and I heard about him on the radio. His story was riveting. He lost his mother and had survived a five-day, 17,000 acre forest fire in the Lincoln National Forest in New Mexico. Firefighters found little Smokey clinging to a burned tree. His paws were burned. He was all alone. His recovery was a popular story, and when they photographed him with a ranger hat on his head, he became the very symbol of protecting forests from forest fires. When Smokey told us that animals are killed in forest fires, I knew I had to act.

Since I was only in second grade and couldn't actually get to his forest to help, I decided I could raise money for his cause. So, one morning, I carefully placed a bandana in my pocket and walked to school with a plan. I told the kids at school that Smokey needed our help and took up a collection of pennies, nickels and dimes and placed them happily in the bandana for Smokey. But when the teacher found out what I had done, I was in trouble. She told my parents and made me give all the money back. I was humiliated and confused. How could it be wrong to try to help Smokey and all the little animals who would get burned in fires if we didn't do anything? I was an extraordinarily shy kid and my idea to ask for money seemed daunting to me, but my innocent, and not totally-programmed heart gave me the strength to do it.

It was the 1950's in Kansas City. World War II was over, and while there was hope in the air for better times, extreme conformity, not innocent hearts, was thought necessary for survival. The teacher was doing what she thought was best for me. If I strayed too far from the status quo, I could be ostracized from the tribe.

For many centuries, the fires of patriarchy that had been oppressing women, children, animals, nature and people considered "other," were burning hotter than any forest fire could. In the name of anthropocentrism and power, just a little over 100 years ago women were hanged or burned to death for allegedly being witches; Native peoples were and continue to be tortured and murdered by the millions. Wars, slavery, and animal agriculture have all been justified by the belief that those at the top have the right to dominate and exploit all those below them. So, from my teacher's view, I would have a better chance of survival, especially as a girl, if I didn't call attention to myself or try to change anything.

My teacher had her own pain, I'm sure, as she had been programmed and probably traumatized into accepting the patriarchal, dominator mindset. She had shut down her wise heart in order to survive in a world of violence and uncertainty. But we children—fans of Smokey and all the animals in the forest—knew that the animals and the trees needed our help. Cultural conditioning had not closed our hearts yet.

"Humility and reverence before the world" There has always been a stirring among human hearts, a calling from deep within us, drawing us ever upward toward a truer way of being. Perhaps our species took a wrong turn and entered the hellish bloody world of anthropocentrism by accident or, more likely, out of fear. Or maybe we've had to endure this adolescent phase before we could understand who we are. But the time is up now. We cannot go on in this reckless, prideful way any longer. Wendell Berry said, "For I do not doubt that it is only on the condition of humility and reverence before the world that our species will be able to remain in it."

My children and grandchildren—treasures of my heart—I want them to be able to "remain in it." How can I—how can we—keep letting it all burn down around them? And the children and grandchildren of the trees and the cows and the wolves? This is a spiritual calling for us to see the world through new eyes; to bear witness to the suffering of the millions of animals, both wild and captive, being slaughtered every hour of every single day; to bear witness to the dead zones in the seas and dead bird's stomachs filled with trash. It hurts to look, I know, because the witnessing child within each one of us is kind and wants to help if a friend is in pain.

There is an answer to all this. It is there waiting for us, giving us, perhaps, one last glorious chance. We have a new story and a new name. We are Homo Ahimsa. We always were, but we lost our way. It's time to embrace ourselves and each other and all beings with this epiphany, this new story. We are Homo Ahimsa. We are the gentle, nonviolent compassionate lovers of all life. We are treasuring and celebrating all life on this sacred place of love called Earth.

May all my sacred brothers and sisters
Walk, fly, swim, and move, in love, peace and freedom.[6]

CHAPTER THREE

Time's Up. We Are At the Crossroads.
Which Path Will We Choose?

*Seven generations after contact with the Europeans
the Onkwehonwe would see the day when the elm
trees would die...Huge stone monsters would tear
open the face of the earth. The rivers would burn.
The air would burn the eyes of man...
the birds would fall from the sky.
The fish would die in the water.
And man would grow ashamed of
the way that he had treated his
Mother and Provider, the Earth.*
Mohawk Prophecy[1]

The warning bells are ringing. Scientists, philosophers, agitators, hippies, prophets, indigenous peoples, and truth seekers have been warning us for decades. In 1980, approximately 12,000 people from around the world camped in tipis and tents at the Black Hills International Survival Gathering in South Dakota, near missile silos stocked with nuclear warheads. Throughout the week-long event, Native Americans and others spoke powerfully of our need to take grass-roots action to stop governments and corporations from continuing to desecrate our sacred Mother Earth. They spoke of the disastrous consequences of nuclear weapons and power plants, the dangers of overhead electric transmission lines, the insanity of mining for uranium, and the need to restore the treaty claims for the Sioux nations. Evenings were filled with famous singers inspiring everyone to get to work, including the highly motivating "Custer Died for Your Sins."

Since then, the assaults on Mother Earth, Native Americans, all animals and all people have only intensified, in spite of valiant attempts by millions of caring people to stop the marauding hordes of the power elite. Why?

> *As long as people will shed the blood of innocent*
> *creatures, there can be no peace, no liberty,*
> *no harmony between people.*
> *Slaughter and justice cannot dwell together.*
> Isaac Bashevis Singer

Revealing the missing key: In all the honorable attempts by the peace, environmental, and social justice movements, there was a key element to success often overlooked. That very important, absolutely essential key was animal agriculture. As Tolstoy famously said, "As long as there are slaughterhouses, there will be battlefields." Once the modern animal rights movement began in earnest in the 1970's, that missing piece was revealed. In spite of massive resistance from the monstrously wealthy animal agriculture industry, as well as individuals who do not want to be told what to eat, the truth is now, finally, squarely in front of us all.

As has been noted, but cannot be repeated too often, Homo Sapiens' craving for animal flesh has enriched and grown the monster of Big Ag until it can now claim to be the major cause behind deforestation, world hunger, the sixth extinction, desertification, erosion, air and water pollution, depleted water tables, habitat and biodiversity loss, social injustice, pandemics and a long list of diseases.

Marching in San Francisco in 2003 with 250,000 other people demanding that we not go to war in Iraq felt real and hopeful. Millions more protested in marches around the world with us.

But the U.S. military industry declared war anyway. There was money and power at stake. Millions of people's pleas for peace were ignored.

In separate marches around the world, millions of people have also protested the endless war against animals. We cannot afford to march separately any more. We cannot have world peace and halt our race to extinction until we stop the war against animals.

> *The human cycle of violence will not stop until*
> *we stop the underlying violence,*
> *the remorseless violence we*
> *commit against animals for food.*
> Will Tuttle

Animal liberation is now everyone's business. We have finally arrived at a pivotal point in time when even those who don't particularly care about animals and their rights to be free from human-caused suffering, have to work now to bring an end to animal agriculture. It is an omnipresent threat to everyone's and our children's survival. But what is beautiful and exciting about all these groups for justice that have been working separately until now, is that by working together we can eliminate this behemoth that is destroying the ecosystems of everyone. We cannot wait for government and industry to become compassionate. But we *can* stop buying and eating their foods of violence and engaging in activities that exploit animals. We can each eat plant-based from this day forward and cause this industry to collapse, as it must. By finding ourselves so empowered and rising to our true nature as Homo Ahimsa, we can replace the other gargantuan engines of destruction as well, such as Big Pharma and the Military Industrial Complex, because we won't need them.

We use the word "replace," because, as Homo Ahimsa, dedicated to non-harm, we will not use violence to stop them. Instead, we will transform in such a way that we will not need these systems that have attempted to program us into believing that we cannot survive without them. As Buckminster Fuller famously said, "You never change things by fighting the existing reality. To change something, build a new model that makes the existing model obsolete." Homo Ahimsa knows how to live, demonstrate, and be the "new model." Homo Ahimsa is Gandhi's "change we want to see in the world."

Predictions of peace on earth and love for all beings: Paramahansa Yogananda once predicted that the world would be vegetarian by 2050. He taught that "Only spiritual conscious-ness—realization of God's presence in oneself and in every other living being—can save the world. I see no chance for peace without it." Of course, due to the situation we are now witness-ing, we need an earlier target date than 2050. He was talking about becoming what we are calling Homo Ahimsa, that is, realizing God or the Divine within us and every other being. Once we realize that, how can we do harm to anyone?

Teilhard de Chardin, philosopher and priest, had great faith in humanity and taught that we are spiritual beings having a human experience. Therefore, we are well-equipped to leave behind the path of violence and become the kind human, whose purpose is to *be love* here on earth. His idea was for all of us to "move ever upward toward greater consciousness and greater love" and that Divine Grace is with us assisting in this transformation. Thomas Jackson, director of the inspiring documentary film, *A Prayer for Compassion*, agrees. He assures us there are "unseen forces on our side."

Teilhard described our glorious transformation in this way: "The people of your time, toward the end of this century [the 20th] will be taking the tiller of the world... It is there that the *noosphere*, the field of mind, will awaken, and we will rebuild the earth... The present chaos is not the end of the world, but the labor pains of a new earth, and a new humanity coming into new form."

Renowned environmental activist, Joanna Macy, phrases it this way, "The most remarkable feature of this historical moment on Earth is not that we are on the way to destroying the world; we've actually been on the way for quite a while. It is that we are beginning to wake up, as from a millennia-long sleep, to a whole new relationship to our world, to ourselves and each other."[2]

Sailesh Rao tells us, with certainty and passion, that we have arrived at a time when we have no choice. We have to create a Vegan World by 2026. This is, as he humorously puts it, "a Holy Shift moment."

Jean Houston speaks of this as "Jump Time;" Willis Harman predicts the "Global Mind Change;" Amma, the "hugging saint" calls us to the "Awakening of Universal Motherhood;" and David Korten pleads for "The Great Turning."

When Woodstock shocked the world in 1969 with its unpredicted crowds of half a million kids and music that challenged the power elite, a wellspring of hope erupted among the people there. When the organizers realized they could not sell tickets after the fences fell and people just kept coming, they announced that everyone could stay whether they had tickets or not. They relinquished their desire for profit at that moment, and the audience got a glimpse of what that kind of sharing could look like. It brought the dream of a world of love, peace, and rock-and-roll a little closer. With the same heart of generosity, Wavy Gravy and the "Hog Farm" stepped up to feed thousands of people free food and keep the peace with the "Please Force." It was an historic turning in its own right. It sent a message to the world that there are a lot of us who are continuing the noble tradition of questioning authority, customs, traditions, business models, and repressive governments. And a lot of that questioning was done with music and fun.

As Joni Mitchell later wrote and sang:

By the time I got to Woodstock
They were half a million strong.
Everywhere there were songs and celebration;
And I dreamed I saw the bombers
Riding shotgun in the sky,
Turning into butterflies
Above our nation.
We are stardust, we are golden,
And we've got to get ourselves back to the garden.

Although bombers did not turn into butterflies, several near butterfly events did actually come out of the sky. The first was a military helicopter circling the crowd. The crowd's reaction initially was fear, but fears turned to joy when it was announced that it was not deployed to use force against them. Rather it was a U.S. Army Medical Corps helicopter that ultimately made multiple landings at Woodstock to bring medical personnel, food and supplies and to transport some concert goers who needed care. The second butterfly happening was the gift of fresh cut flowers dropped from an Army helicopter. "Everyone started screaming with joy. It felt like a dream…of what this world could be, people helping one another, loving one another, no matter our differences."[3] These were unexpected, enthralling symbols of hope, showing us that human beings can live without violence.

So here we are at this crossroads. Do we believe enough in ourselves? We have to make a choice. And the choice is more obvious and compelling than it has ever been. The situation we are in was caused by Homo Sapiens, with all its misconceptions and unconscious ideas about who we are. Homo Sapiens, as it operates now, cannot solve the problems it has created. But living by our highest ideals of love and nonviolence and awakening to our true nature, we can solve the problems in ways we have dreamed and ways we have not yet dreamed. Are we ready to choose that path? Do we believe it's possible? Can we let go of our old programmed identities and patriarchal belief systems? If we can, we have a chance!

A challenging question hangs in the air. *Are human beings capable of being nonviolent?* Our ancestors, our parents, and we have all been programmed from birth to believe that we are predatory creatures who must compete with other people and animals to get what we want. Governments, religions, schools, and the workplace reinforce this ideology continually. Being at the bottom of the hierarchy is bad; being at the top means success. There are wars of physical aggression with chemicals, missiles, mines, and guns. Others involve cyber-attacks and economic strangleholds. Secretive government takeovers in order to control the minerals, oil, and land of vulnerable countries are the modern forms of invasion and empire expansion. There seem to be aggression and predation everywhere. So how can there be any hope?

War is a new invention, and its twin is animal agriculture. In his 2007 book, *Beyond War: The Human Potential for Peace*, anthropologist Douglas Fry takes a refreshing look at ancient cultures, as well as contemporary simple gatherer-hunter bands, who lived or currently live fairly harmoniously without apparent evidence of ever having gone to war. Like the women anthropologists we will read about in Chapter Four, who discovered that male anthropologists' interpretations of some ancient cultures were tainted by their own patriarchal biases, Fry notes much of the same bias in interpretations of war. By carefully examining the archaeological and anthropological reports of small gatherer-hunter groups (that is, people who do or did not use agriculture or use it minimally), he found that many of these groups had been categorized as warlike, even though they had never waged war. The data showed that individual acts of violence, such as the murder of one person by another person and feuding for personal reasons, were erroneously included under the heading of war.

To clear up the confusion, Fry uses the word "war" to mean what most people would agree is a good definition: "relatively impersonal lethal aggression between communities."[4] By including homicide under the heading of war, anthropologists, operating out of their own bias of man as a violent warrior, made many gatherer-hunter groups appear much more aggressive than they really were. Fry points out that these groups were nomadic, did not build fortresses, did not have weapons of war, were egalitarian, not hierarchical, and men and women were equally respected. Moreover, and very importantly, while there were certain members who were greatly admired for their wisdom or abilities, they did not have any authority to force people into battle. It makes perfect sense that cooperation, sharing with other groups, and respecting each other's autonomy was good for survival. If you have found water in an area and share it with a nearby group this year, then next year, if you run short, the group you shared with will now share their water with you. Fighting over the water could lead to injuries and death, and every member of the clan is important to the survival of the group. So fighting does not make good sense.

By studying archaeological clues from the far distant past and anthropological findings from contemporary gathering bands, Fry draws a convincing hypothesis that war is a very recent phenomenon. It will not be to our surprise to see that war, as we think of it now and as Fry defines it, was born along with animal agriculture around 10,000 years ago. Confining animals made it possible for the populations of humans to grow in size. An entirely new way of living in the world commenced. Animal agriculture opened the Pandora's box of violence and war, and led us to where we are today.

While small nomadic bands likely lived with no knowledge of or desire for war, the new animal agriculturalists became mired in it. Egalitarianism was replaced by hierarchies. The more aggressive people in the groups saw the potential to accumulate wealth. By forcing others to supply them with food and weapons, build fortresses, and go to war, they could amass more land, wealth and power. Chronically overlooked by anthropologists is the influence that confining and killing animals for food had on the psyches of the people. The cultural systems that developed around such aggression seemed to prove that certain men are superior to all others, especially animals, and must be obeyed.

As Dr. Will Tuttle explains, these new sedentary populations, "were oriented around meat eating, herding, slavery, violent conquest, male supremacy, and offering animal sacrifices to their mostly male gods."[5] Tuttle notes that the Latin root of the word "capital" is "capita" which means head. In ancient times, wealth was measured in the numbers of animals owned. This quest for more capital, of course, led to fierce wars to acquire more land for herding and confining animals. The lust for wealth, and the animal agriculture that fed it, became the template upon which patriarchy increasingly dominated life on the planet in ever widening paths of destruction and cruelty.

It is not easy to grasp the significance of this apparent alteration in human behavior from cooperative partners to competitive dominators. We have all grown up with written history describing humanity as violent and warlike. But historical writings prior to the time of agriculture are rare. So, by the time people began documenting historical events in earnest, the hierarchical, patrilineal, dominator way of life was well-established. It paints a picture of humanity as innately violent and full of evil intent. The Bible, and many other early written records, are overflowing with tales of war, animal sacrifice, human sacrifice, slavery, and stomach-churning acts of violence. If it were not for the archaeological findings of people who apparently lived without war in partnership style for many centuries and anthropological studies of a few living indigenous groups, we would not know that war is relatively recent and that we are not doomed to be "man, the warrior."

And yet, in these same written records of the last few thousand years, there are many rays of light. The values of the Golden Rule, as we will find in Chapter 6, kept popping up in many cultures, religions, and philosophies. The violent lust for wealth could not completely obscure the human longing for love and cooperation, the desire for living in partnership, and, perhaps, some dim, collective memory of a peaceful garden somewhere.

> *We need never look for universal peace on this*
> *earth until men stop killing animals for food.*
> *The lust for blood has permeated the race*
> *thought and the destruction of life will continue*
> *to repeat its psychology, the world round, until men*
> *willingly observe the law in all phases of life,*
> *"Thou shalt not kill."*
> Charles Fillmore, "The Vegetarian," May 1920[6]

In the immortal words of airline attendants everywhere, "We know you have many airlines to choose from. Thank you for choosing ours." We do have choices at this troubled time in history. Number one: we can give up in the face of the enormity of it all. Number two: we can do nothing and hope the government and corporations will fix this in time. Or Number three: we can travel together as Homo Ahimsa and turn this crisis into an opportunity to finally create peace and bring Heaven to Earth for all. Let's fly on Number three.

CHAPTER FOUR

Silent No More. The Divine Mother
in Us All Rises from the Ashes

"Nevertheless, she persisted." Without intending to do so, U.S. Senator Mitch McConnell inadvertently gave the women of the world an empowering new mantra in 2017. Senator Elizabeth Warren began reading a letter from Coretta Scott King on the Senate floor as part of her opposition to the appointment of Jeff Sessions as Attorney General. McConnell interrupted her and demanded she "take her seat." "She was warned," he intoned with unsurprising hubris, "she was given an explanation. Nevertheless, she persisted." Those last three words are now emblazoned on t-shirts, coffee cups, protest signs and bumper stickers. The oft repeated order to sit down and be quiet has been an abuse to women for thousands of years. But women are silent no more.

We are witnessing the advent of an age in which the domination of women is coming to an end. The #MeToo movement is a green-light indicator that women have had enough male supremacy and are through with it forever. We really don't need any more evidence that the system of domination by those in power only leads to ruin. And let's be very clear. We are not suggesting we switch to a matriarchy. That would simply be another hierarchical form of domination and power over others. The imaginal vision of our new way of living is based on the partnership model, as opposed to the domination model. It is up to each one of us to bring that way of living into being in every possible way. We need to take an inventory of our own programmed ideas about human beings, animals, and the earth. We have been trapped in the old, toxic and violent worldview long enough.

The good news is that we are beginning to awaken to the fact that—without the feminine, divine mother energy being embraced—we face continued and endless violence. This has profound implications for animals. It is just one more step up in consciousness to further comprehend that, as long as we are killing animals, no matter how much respect women gain, we will never pull ourselves out of the bloody mire of patriarchal destruction. It will maintain its power as long as we allow the domination, abuse, raping, robbing, and killing of our animal cousins.

Misogyny and mass shootings: Patriarchy may be in its death throes, but it is not gone yet. A serial killer took the lives of six people in 2014 in a California town. The day before that, he posted a video in which he railed against women, claiming that they were torturing him with sexual deprivation. He promised to get revenge against women for this. Chillingly, this person had an online following of people who revered him for his rage at women, celebrated other mass killings, and wrote about doing the same, themselves.

Jillian Peterson founded The Violence Project which studies mass shootings. "'They're angry and they're suicidal and they've had traumatic childhoods and these hard lives, and they get to a point and they find something or someone to blame....'" she explains. "For some people, that is women, and we are seeing that kind of take off.'" She believes there is a link between misogyny and mass shootings.[1]

There are about ninety-five male prisoners to every five incarcerated women worldwide. U.S. statistics appear to hover around ninety-one men to nine women prisoners. Helpinggangyouth. com estimates that 90 to 94% of gang members are male. At the same time, approximately 80% of animal activists are women. There is also a gender gap between men and women who give of their time without pay to volunteer for many different organizations from grade schools to civic and activist organizations. In exploring this, Dan Kopf found that "...even when we only compare men and women who work full-time, we still find a large gender gap in terms of who volunteers... when it comes to demonstrating altruism through volunteering,... Regardless of whether they work or not, how old they are, or how rich they are, women just volunteer more."[2]

This great disparity between the sexes is another tragic result of the toxic mindset that forces men into artificial roles that deny their innate feminine nature. Because they perceive the culture as eminently exploitative, they sense that they must compete to find their place in the highly unstable and frightening hierarchy of other males. Cultures have taught them for thousands of years to hide their tears and their feelings of compassion. They must toughen up and "be a man." They are shamed if they "throw like a girl," "run like a girl," or do anything that appears feminine. Many coaches, teachers, and parents who are unconsciously indoctrinated into the cultural bias, that men are intrinsically better than women, unwittingly play a part in programming young boys into this destructive and violent mindset.

Our demand for more of everything could lead us to the end of everything. This anthropocentric conditioning has been going on since animal agriculture began. The balance that is possible between the sacred feminine and the sacred masculine has been severely compromised for millennia. Without doubt, all species and all of glorious nature have suffered under this fear-based oppression and confusion. This highly problematic concept of the world is causing the blood-thirsty killing of billions of incarcerated animals, the collapse of ecosystems and the mass extinction of wild species. *In perhaps the greatest irony ever displayed by* *humanity, our demand for more of everything could lead us to the end of everything.*

Could the lesson be any more obvious? We have to stop our reckless, abusive behavior and transform spiritually. We have to grow up and *be* Homo Ahimsa, bring balance to the masculine and feminine energies, release our ravaging caterpillar existence, search our "imaginal cells" for the truth of who we are, and become the healing butterflies that bring beauty and life to the planet.

Churches subverting patriarchy: Yale Divinity School's Journal recently focused intensely on "Sex, Gender, Power: A Reckoning." The bulk of the journal articles dealt with subverting patriarchy and male domination and about creating new ways for people of all genders to see each other as equals. Marie Fortune, an ethics theologian, writes, "#MeToo has intensified the moral accounting. Every denomination now faces its own reckoning. Survivors are silent no more."[3] For far too long, she explains, all the unconscious programming that patriarchy has injected into society has allowed sexual violence to go on without any meaningful ethical argument.

In other words, since we live in a patriarchal world, sexual violence is regarded as normal—"boys will be boys." She points out that, although we have made some progress, "We are still living with a version of male sexuality that assumes entitlement to sexual access to vulnerable women, men, children, and youth, with the expectation that such acts of sexual abuse and exploitation by powerful people will be ignored and covered up by other powerful people." She calls patriarchy "the air we breathe. And it is toxic for us all." She wants to deconstruct the "patriarchal pillars of our faith traditions" and "make the church a place where those victimized by sexual violence can come for justice and healing, not rejection and belittling."[4]

The 1963 song "Wives and Lovers," by Jack Jones, reveals the tragic message women and girls, not to mention men, were receiving at that time and right up to the present. A portion of the lyrics tells the tale: "...Run to his arms the moment he comes home to you. I'm warning you. Day after day, there are girls at the office, and men will always be men. Don't send him off with your hair still in curlers. You may not see him again..."

Betty married her husband in 1940 after receiving her college degree. It took a strong woman to go to college then, especially since many professional jobs were not available for women, once they graduated and married. Most employers expected married women to have children and could freely discriminate against them without any consequence. When Betty discovered that her husband was having multiple affairs from the beginning of the marriage, her mother told her, "You made your bed, so you have to lie in it." Other friends, many of whom were experiencing the same heartache, told her that's just what men do. It was considered normal. She stayed in the marriage for 25 years, until *he* left *her* for another woman ("at the office.")

Multiple women patients, including one as young as 15, found themselves in the office of a psychologist who was a sexual predator. Although several attempted to get justice, the only result for one woman was a private civil suit which did not result in imprisonment for the crime. His insurance company paid the bill. Eventually, after enough complaints, the regulatory board quietly took his license to practice psychotherapy but allowed him to practice psychology in other ways. Citing poor health, the real reasons were swept under the rug. Like so many Catholic priests, Boy Scout leaders, ministers and others, whose predatory behaviors were tolerated and allowed to go unchecked, most of these men in powerful positions have been protected by their organizations and lived out their lives facing no justice whatsoever.

Killing animals kills our own sacred feminine. While #Metoo and other efforts are now bringing serious attention to sexual predation and the oppression of vulnerable *human* beings, animal activists are working to show the connection between oppression of human women and our female animal cousins. The same imbalance and oppression of the feminine principle has resulted in the normalizing of the brutal raping and killing of billions upon billions of female animals. As Will Tuttle explains, "The inner feminine is our intuition, our sensitivity, and our ability to sense the profound interconnectedness of events and beings, and it is vital to peace, wisdom, joy, intelligence, creativity, and spiritual awakening. With every baby calf stolen from her mother and killed, with every gallon of milk stolen from enslaved and broken mothers, with every thrust of the raping sperm gun, with every egg stolen from a helpless, frantic hen, and with every baby chick killed or locked for life in a hellish nightmare cage, we kill the sacred feminine within ourselves."[5]

It always goes back to the core belief in domination. All females of all species and all vulnerable beings, including rivers, oceans, forests and jungles, are at the mercy of those who believe it is their right to humiliate, rob, rape, ravage and kill or have others do it for them. The sacred feminine knows how to give love, to give life. That beautiful essence lives in every one of us, but it has been suppressed by our own internal unconscious programs that tell us feminine energy is inferior, weak, stupid, and ineffective.

> *The essence of motherhood is not restricted*
> *to women who have given birth; it is a principle*
> *inherent in both women and men… It is love…*
> *for those in whom motherhood has awakened,*
> *love and compassion towards everyone are*
> *as much part of their being as breathing.*
> Amma, the Hugging Saint[6]

This sacred feminine energy that has for so long been oppressed in both men and women has also been called universal motherhood. Far from being inferior, it embodies the miraculous qualities of nurturing, compassion, empathy, unconditional love and a sense of connectedness to nature and other beings. All people are endowed with the sacred feminine, as are all who have life. Dogs and cats show us what empathy means when they comfort us in our grief or pain. When we walk quietly in the wilderness, the beauty and wonder that embraces us there can bring us to our knees. When we feel the essence and the presence of Mother Earth, as we put our arms around a special tree, we are literally touching the sacred feminine.

Reverend Carol Saunders writes, "When masculine energy is not balanced by feminine, we experience dominance, aggression and action without wisdom. The bottom line is we suffer in the imbalance—all of us, not just women. Men suffer because their Sacred Feminine also yearns for expression. And for those men who are in balance, the out-of-balance world is a difficult place for them to feel belonging."[7]

"We are the granddaughters of the witches they couldn't burn." We are being urgently called to correct this imbalance. With each passing day, with each new travesty caused by the violent cultural belief system, we realize that we can never hope to heal life on Earth by operating from the same mindset that caused this destruction and desecration of all that is holy and beautiful. We are here now to make this right. Together we are here to let the sacred feminine within us rise out of the ashes of all the "witches" and animals and forests who have been burned to death while our feminine nature was barely breathing. We must let her nourish us, heal us and teach us the way of beauty, universal motherhood, infinite compassion, and selfless, unconditional love. With Homo Ahimsa living in balance, we— both men and women—can be the midwives who birth this new world into being. Being Homo Ahimsa embodies both the sacred masculine and the sacred feminine in glorious balance. Vegan living is the perfect expression of that. It is time to honor and uplift the presence of the divine feminine within each one of our souls and within every tree and flower and bee and cow. The sacred feminine within us is not a killer. It is a healer.

Lessons from the Partnership cultures of prehistory: Amy Peck writes about how restricted and handicapped we have all been under the violent power of domination. "Unfortunately," she notes, "seeing the vast, infinite, absolute and indescribable Goddessence only in the form of masculine metaphor and symbol has severely limited our human spiritual potential and greatly hindered our ability to live in peace and balance on this earth."[8]

Peck, like many others, is now pointing to a distant past in which men and women lived for thousands of years in egalitarian societies that did not experience war. The 1987 book by Riane Eisler, *The Chalice and the Blade*, revealed to the public an entirely new look at some ancient civilizations. She theorized that male anthropologists and archaeologists had misinterpreted artifacts from prehistoric Neolithic and Paleolithic eras. She reported that, as more women joined the anthropology profession, an entirely new picture of these cultures came into view. The women scientists found evidence that, what the male scientists had seen through the lens of patriarchy as sexual objects, were instead evidence of matrilineal, peaceful, egalitarian cultures. Eisler calls them partnership communities, as opposed to dominator groups. As we discussed in Chapter 3, the bands that Fry described apparently lived in relative peace without any indication of war for thousands of years. Men and women were equally respected, and there was evidence of well-being for all members of the communities.[9]

If the Pandora's box of confining and killing animals had never been opened, perhaps we would be living far different lives today.

Such brutal farming practices allowed wealth to accumulate in the hands of a few. That wealth, of course, made possible the hierarchies of kings and priests. As their greed and demand for power grew, wars, slavery, disease, pandemics, plagues and vicious cruelty became the story of humanity, and the apparent peace of prehistoric peoples, who did not leave a complex written history, faded into the mists of time.

Spirit, logic, and ethics all tell us that we cannot have justice and respect for women as long as we are raping, robbing, and taking away the babies of mothers of other species. We cannot have peace among people as long as we deny it to all other living beings. We cannot heal our mother earth as long as we enslave, trap, poison, and kill her children. We cannot live by religious proclamations that refuse to honor all God's creation, nor can we follow the guidance of spiritual teachers who claim enlightenment while ordering the massive killing of innocent, sacred beings for their meals, entertainment, and clothing.

The simple truth is inescapable. We have the obvious mental and physical ability to commit horrors that only the human brain can imagine and carry out. We see the consequences of that fierce and pointless aggression. We are now reaping what has been sown for ten thousand years of brutality, and we have no choice. We have to stop the insanity.

It took us thousands of years to get to this cliff over which we are now looking, but the time is up. Lessons have been learned. Many experiments in living have been tried. The blessing is that, by process of elimination, *we now know what to do.* We have discovered through trial and error what our true destiny is. We are not just partners with other people. We are partners with all sacred life. We have within us holy masculine and feminine intuition; we have within us the capacity and, indeed, the longing to end our violent way of living, to stop being the blood-thirsty consumers of animal flesh, to stop the destruction of ecosystems and the massive extinction of wild animals. It is our true heart; it is our true spirit. If we ask people if they would purposefully harm an animal, nearly all will say they would not. Deep within, they are already vegan, already longing to reveal their true ahimsa nature.

We are Homo Ahimsa awakening! We are bringing the feminine mothering powers of humility, lovingkindness, healing, wisdom, protectiveness, empathy, and compassion into complete expression. These qualities will no longer acquiesce to commands to sit down and be quiet. Instead, these values will lead humanity from domination to true partnership, from so-called Sapiens to real Ahimsa.

PART TWO: HOW

How to Transcend to Our True
Nature as Homo Ahimsa;
Let Go of the Dominator Worldview;
And Live in Partnership, Reverence,
Nonviolence and Gratitude with All Life

CHAPTER FIVE

How Do We See and Know Our Inner Ahimsa?

Overcome evil with good and falsehood
with truth and hatred with love.
Peace Pilgrim

Nourishing our spiritual lives helps us see and know that we already *are* Homo Ahimsa. Nearly all social justice movements have been rooted in the spiritual quest to create a better world—one that includes everyone as equals and is nonviolent. It is selfless love that shouts from our spirits—we must do something to make things right. But how does spirituality help us reach our higher nature?

Our spirits can give us strength and faith that we *can* and *will* create a vegan, nonviolent world of peace. With mutual support from like-minded and spirited friends, and faith in the Abiding Love of the Universe, we can find the strength to overcome compassion fatigue, face the suffering of the world, and continue this work. We need to *be* together to develop mindfulness, inner peace, and feel the joy, gratitude and grace of living as Homo Ahimsa.

The power of intention, focused thought, and prayer, springing out of unconditional love for all life is, according to Gandhi and many other wise spiritual activists, the most powerful force on earth. By adding these to our liberation actions, we create an energy field of compassion and love that is felt by activists, animals, and people worldwide.

We can be assured that in mysterious ways, our prayers do indeed bring comfort to the Earth and to the people and animals suffering under the current regime of domination. With our prayers and intentions, we bathe the energy field of the world with compassion. This touches hearts and souls with the awareness that people everywhere are working for freedom and healing for all. These prayers and intentions also help to elevate global consciousness and hasten the emergence of Homo Ahimsa in all people. Through this spiritual aspect of animal and human liberation work, we are helping to reveal the true consciousness of compassion, love, cooperation, nonviolence, and reverence for all life that already dwells in all human hearts. The heart of humanity longs to be set free from the bondage of the domination paradigm under which we have labored for so long.

It is essential that we take time to go within and to spend time in nature in order to feel the ecstatic joy of being alive and being a treasured part of the physical and metaphysical world. With that joy firmly established in our hearts, we feel such a kinship with the earth, the plants, animals and people that we no longer want to cause harm. As we arrive on this solid ground of reverence for ourselves and all life, we realize we cannot participate in killing and destroying whether it is done directly or indirectly. We reveal ourselves as Homo Ahimsa, finally, fully aware of who we are. And with that awareness comes, not only the joy, but also the intuitive clarity of what to do. Each one of us has something amazing to bring to this new world of harmony and balance. Each one of us has a special gift to give that springs from the ecstasy and gratitude we feel and the vision we hold of a liberated and healed world.

By ethical conduct toward all creatures,
we enter into a spiritual relationship with the universe.
Dr. Albert Schweitzer

The word "spirituality" can trigger negative reactions among us. There are many of us who have a knee-jerk reaction against the word "spirituality." That word often triggers bad memories or thoughts about religion. Many places of worship, as we are painfully aware, ignore the worldwide plight of animals and, in fact, openly exploit them at potlucks, fishing and hunting outings, rodeos, zoos, circuses, and other "traditional" family activities. Many of us have found ourselves frustrated when we tried working to change their policies to be cruelty-free and animal and environmentally friendly, as well as inclusive of all people. In addition, we all know sincere people, who may not attend a place of worship, but consider themselves spiritual seekers. Many of them participate in all the socially programmed rituals of animal abuse and killing. They may be exploring Buddhism, attending retreats, practicing yoga, studying shamanism, and/or reading spiritual books. But they have not yet made the connection between their desire to be spiritual and the need to live nonviolently.

Beyond the mind: In many ways, activists and change-makers who resist the term "spiritual" are spiritual even though they don't like the term. They are spiritual because they are compelled to do this selfless work. It is not just because of mental logic that they long for a better world. Rather it is because they have gone beyond the mind to spirit. It is in our spirits that we find the upwelling of passion to make the world better. Spirituality is what we feel and deeply know in our hearts, far out beyond the mind and logic. If you care about the suffering of others, in spite of society's pressure to ignore it, you are a person who is in touch with your true heart and your true spirit. Spirituality is the unseen, but deeply felt, *ahimsa love* that dwells naturally in your hearts. In that sense, you have truly been called by the Spirit of Love to do what you can to help liberate animals and nature from human tyranny and liberate humanity from the corruption of patriarchy. *And* you have answered the call.

If you are living a vegan life already, then you have heard your soul's call to align your actions with your heart's desire to do the least harm and the most good. It is in perfect accord with the vow of ahimsa by which Gandhi lived. That Sanskrit word is so rich in meaning. It embraces noninjury, selfless service, divine love, nonviolence, compassion, reverence for all life. Surely, these are highest and best guideposts for living. Gandhi took the vow of ahimsa and demonstrated its radiant power and beauty throughout his life. It says "no" to all harm, and "yes" to life and love. Let us stop for a moment, take a deep breath, and *see, really see,* a world full of Homo Ahimsas. What a thrilling vision!

> *Every leaf of the tree becomes a page of the*
> *sacred scripture once the soul has learned to read.*
> Saadi of Shariz, medieval Persian Sufi poet and mystic

From vegetarianism and pacifism to unfettered brutality: Charles Vaclavik writes extensively about how Jesus' teachings of vegetarianism, communalism and pacifism were upended by the Catholic church. The Catholic church was so-named because the word "catholic" means universal. The goal of Catholicism was to build on the already wildly popular idea of anthropocentrism and create a church that could gain so much political power that it could rule the world. Vaclavik recounts, "Under the auspices of the Christian Church, armies plundered the Holy Land, killing and slaughtering those human beings who were not Christian. The Crusades can hardly be rationally explained, let alone justified, when viewed from the perspective of the gentle Jesus. The Crusades…were pure unadulterated aggression…"[1] The savage Inquisition which lasted for over six hundred years was only part of the brutality of the church. The invasion of the Americas, to steal the wealth there, was unapologetically supported by the Catholic hierarchy, leading to the torture and death of millions of native peoples. Even though Jesus taught compassion, equality, and nonviolence, the Catholic Christians of those early days made certain that the Bible contained verses that justified slavery and all manner of cruel exploitation and killing of others.

When Thomas Paine gave his review of the Bible in his "Age of Reason," he declared, "It is a history of wickedness, that has served to corrupt and brutalize mankind; and, for my part, I sincerely detest it as I detest everything that is cruel."

Keith Akers points out in his books on Jesus' life, that Jesus was not trying to establish a new religion. He grew up in a Jewish family and community that believed in simple living, vegetarianism and pacifism. These people were against the animal sacrifice that many Jews of the time subscribed to, and Jesus made that clear when he drove the animals out of the Temple. Akers clarifies for us that the larger Christian church eventually overpowered the teachings of Jesus. "The values of simple living and nonviolence became increasingly marginalized in a church that came to accept the very materialism and violence against which Jesus had protested."[2] The values and beliefs of the followers of Jesus were quite literally rejected, both by the pro-sacrifice Jews and by the Christians of that era.

Pythagoras, the Greek philosopher who lived some 500 years before Jesus, taught vegetarianism, wore no wool, opposed the pursuit of wealth, and opposed slavery and animal sacrifice. He taught his followers that they must not harm their enemies or cause suffering to animals. It is quite possible that Jesus' community was influenced by Pythagoras' teachings for hundreds of years before Jesus was born.

Many other religions and ethical philosophies have also experienced the same fate as Christianity. Like the Pythagoreans who understood the divine insight that we are here to love all creation, all life, and not to destroy it, many of these schools of thought were rooted in reverence for life. The wellspring of such thinking was spiritual—human beings somehow tapping into transcendent wisdom that we are not on this earth to dominate and destroy. Yet, as we know, most of these became organized into religions that left their spiritual roots behind and went on to actually assist in the justification of human violence.

Rama Ganesan notes that while many Indians are vegetarian, often the reason is centered on the self, because killing an animal creates bad karma. "Veganism," she writes, "is recognizing and respecting the lives of other animals, which is different from merely refraining from killing animals for the sake of your own karma." She notes that there are such labels as "ahimsa silk" and "ahimsa milk," leading to the conclusion that it is ok to use animals if you are humane and ahimsaish about it. The word "ahimsa" itself has actually been compromised.[3]

The point is that it is spiritual insight, not compromised, religious dogma, that is leading us now to true wisdom. We now know that the anthropocentric distortion of religion is wrong and has led to some of the greatest evils the world has ever known. It is in our hearts and spirits that the truth shines forth and calls us to create this new and gentle world. Many churches, temples and places of faith are poised, some closer than others, to return to their original truth now because of the dire situation we are all facing. If you do attend a place of worship and are frustrated with the apparent lack of will to stand firm for nonviolence and love, you could be the one to help bring the light into the darkness there. There is a Resources section at the end of the book that lists organizations that can help. If you do not want to attend a place of worship or identify with a distinct religious group, you can form your own Vegan Spirituality group. Help for that is also in the Resources section.

There is a power in spirituality that can be used for the good of all life and to help us bring humanity into its highest expression as Homo Ahimsa. Spirit is that mysterious and metaphysical force or energy that breathes life into our physical bodies. There are scientific explanations for how the physical body works, but none to explain *why*. We know, on some deep level, that when we act in loving ways, in tune with the nearly universal Golden Rule, we feel aligned with our spirits. Our bodies and minds function well when we are in tune with our true nature—love. And they function poorly when we act against the essence of who we are. When we feel an upwelling of love and compassion that moves us deeply, where does it come from? Could it really be just brain matter and hormones causing these feelings? Or could there be a spirit or soul within each one of us that moves us to tears at the sight of anyone suffering, whether that sacred individual is an animal, a person, a flower or the earth?

Father Donatello Iocco experienced a soul awakening to go vegan. Watching the documentary film *Vegucated*, he saw the anguish of a mother cow on a dairy farm running after her baby who had been stolen from her. That was enough to break down the old programs, both cultural and religious. This Catholic priest is now the *vegan* pastor of St. Ambrose church in Toronto. He has courageously found a way to bypass the accepted violence of traditional religion and to discover the truth about the holy sacredness of all life. "As a Christian," he believes, "and a priest, the only way to live our lives in accordance to what we believe is to be vegan. God gave every living being the breath of life. Therefore, all life is sacred no matter what species we are. We believe in a loving and compassionate God who is also merciful. We are called to manifest God's love, compassion and mercy to all of his creation."[4]

Is Veganism a Religion? In a 2013 survey, questions were asked of 165 ethical vegans to determine if ethical veganism is a religion, based on three federal tests of what constitutes a religion. The results determined that ethical veganism does meet the criteria for being a religion under U.S. law.[5]

However, in one important way, veganism is much more than a religion. One of the values people around the world hold dear is the freedom to practice one's own belief system. People of faith have chosen their particular religion because it resonates with them, it feels right, makes sense, and they may even have had an epiphany or religious calling to follow a certain faith. An increasing number of modern religious leaders are encouraging their members to practice tolerance and understanding for people who practice other faiths and to respect their views.

Veganism, rather than being a separate religion, is instead the foundational ideal of nearly all religions. Therefore, this is not about homogenizing religions or about creating a separate religion, but rather it is about helping all the different religions to see that vegan living is the highest expression of the love and non-harm that all faiths hold sacred.

Veganism can be legally considered a religion in the U.S., but vegans are not asking to be tolerated and respected as a distinct group unto themselves. If we ask for that, we are essentially saying that we choose veganism in the same way that someone would choose to be an Episcopalian or a Buddhist. In this day of growing religious tolerance, that leaves the impression that we just want to be treated as fairly as other religions and not be discriminated against. But that is not the mission. It is, rather, to help all religions understand that the very light that shines within all of them is divine love and reverence for all life. And because of the urgency of our times, people of faith are desperately needed to assist in this momentous, radical, and revolutionary transformation of humanity.

This is definitely not a call to a certain religion, at the exclusion of others. This is a call to literally save the Earth and all beings from our collective violence. Slavery abolitionists have come from many different religions. You do not have to be a Baptist to oppose slavery. Civil rights and women's rights activists do not all have to be Catholic or Buddhist. These are issues that call on the best in every person's heart no matter what their religion is. In fact, many, if not all, social justice and peace activists come together to work *in spite* of their religious differences.

As the late Peace and Justice Activist, Father Daniel Berrigan stated, "It is very rare to sustain a movement in recognizable form without a spiritual base." So, by acknowledging our spiritual foundation, the wellspring upon which our dedication thrives, we empower our vision to greater heights and greater possibilities. This is and must be a holistic movement for the bodies, minds, and spirits of us all and of all sacred life.

Helping the billions of people of faith join us to create an ahimsa world: What draws each one of us to dedicate our lives to the liberation of animals, nature and people from human domination and exploitation? It is that deep spiritual knowing that it is wrong to harm and kill and absolutely right to love all beings. That is the rock-solid truth that lives, however hidden, in every human heart and is the foundation, however lost or obscured it may be, for nearly every religion.

By embracing our own spiritual longing to bring more love to the world, we can connect with religious people and those on a spiritual path. Our common ground is the same. We all want to create a better world, and we feel called to do something about it. That passion connects us to each other. It is there at that intersection of love and the will to make the world better that we can meet heart to heart and find our way home.

With the vast majority of people in the world believing in God or a higher power and practicing mindfulness or a chosen faith, getting the message of compassion and the ahimsa partnership model of living to them would bring an earth-shaking, tectonic shift in consciousness. There is great resistance among many of the faithful to this message. Yet, with a little reflection on the true ideals of their religious tradition, it becomes clear that living as Homo Ahimsa is the best possible way to align their highest beliefs with their actions. In doing so, we all honor our own sacred body, honor all God's creatures, heal the beautiful earth, and end violence toward all.

> *There are realms of gold hidden*
> *deep in the human heart.*
> Hindu proverb

The Golden Rule says we can be "Golden." Paul McKenna has created a beautiful Golden Rule poster that is making its way around the world. The poster showcases a collection of Golden Rule statements from many religions. Here are a few of those transformative guidelines:[6]

> Confucianism: What you do not want done
> to yourself, do not do to others
> Analects

> Christianity: Do unto others as you would
> have them do unto you.
> Jesus, Matthew 7:12

> Zoroastrianism: Do not do unto others
> whatever is injurious to yourself.
> Shayast-na-shayast 13.29

> Jainism: One should treat all creatures
> in the world as one would like to be treated.
> Mahavira Sutrakritanga

> Judaism: What is hateful to you, do not do
> to your neighbor. This is the whole
> Torah; all the rest is commentary.
> Hillel, Talmud, Shabbat 31a

> Islam: Not one of you truly believes until
> you wish for others what you wish for yourself.

The Prophet Muhammad, Hadith

Hinduism: This is the sum of duty:
do not do to others what would
cause pain if done to you.
Mahabharata 5:1517

Buddhism: Treat not others in ways
that you yourself would find hurtful.
The Buddha, Udana-Varga 5:18

These are just a few of the many golden rules espoused by nearly every religion and ethical philosophy. This tells us something amazing about Homo Sapiens. These are nearly universal ideals, worldwide insights into who we really are and what we really believe about our place in the world. So far, we have been falling short of who we want to be. But just as the oak tree lives in the acorn, this pattern, this possibility lives in each one of us waiting to sprout and grow.

As Stevie Ray Vaughn sang, "Whatever happened to the Golden Rule?" In spite of the lofty words of this guiding light that few people would reject, we human beings keep stumbling over our fears, unquestioned traditions, and cultural myths, with the universally agreed-upon Golden Rule seemingly just out of reach. Even a cursory look tells us that continuing on our very un-golden path will lead to a very tarnished dead end. Changing course demands that we wake up and question everything that has been programmed into us. If dominating nature, animals, and people has not worked and, if we are really golden beings of love, then our path ahead is crystal clear. Far from being a dead end, it is a new beginning that celebrates life. Our urgent calling now is to transform our actions, thoughts, beliefs, and traditions— everything that causes harm:

• From bullying to nurturing;

- From using and killing animals to giving them freedom from all human exploitation, incarceration, and violence;
- From wars and violence against people and animals to peace and cooperation;
- From commodification of ourselves and other beings to cooperation and reverence for all;
- From fear of others to love of others;
- From desire for power to desire for all to thrive;
- From the violence inherent in animal slaughter to the peace and bliss of veganism;
- And from the diabolical dominator worldview to the passionate partnership way of life.

To be free, we must practice freeing others.
To feel loved, we must practice loving others.
To have true self-respect, we must respect others.
The animals and other voiceless beings,
the starving humans and future generations,
are pleading with us to see: it's on our plate.[7]
Dr. Will Tuttle

Vegan living is the Golden Rule in Action. It is the blueprint for the partnership way of life. It is the opposite of the dominator way of life. It is a vow from the heart to do the least harm and the most good for everyone we meet, no matter the species, gender, nationality, or belief system. Living that way reveals our true nature and leads us forward to our higher level of consciousness and love.

In 1889, Charles and Myrtle Fillmore founded the Unity church. They also established the Unity Inn in Kansas City which was a vegetarian restaurant, when vegetarianism was an oddity in the central U.S. The Fillmores wrote a Unity Statement of Faith which included this: "We believe that all life is sacred and that man should not kill or be a party to the killing of animals for food; also that cruelty, war, and wanton destruction of human life will continue so long as men destroy animals." Myrtle died in 1931, and as Charles aged (making his transition in 1948) others took over the management of the church. But the new staff had not grasped the genius of the Fillmores. Because the new leaders were lost in anthropocentric thinking, they removed that essential and all-important Statement of Faith in 1939. The spirit and truth of that critical statement was pushed underground, in the same way that women and so many others were silenced. As if by prophesy, World War II began in the same year that the blazing fire of that statement was snuffed out. Wars will continue, the Fillmores proclaimed, "as long as men destroy animals."

The "love one another" Golden Rule is possibly the most revolutionary idea ever conceived by human beings. It asks us to act from our spirit which is unselfish, connected to all life, and not conditioned by culture, tradition or religious dogma. It is the highest ideal for human behavior. While many religious people acknowledge that, indeed, their faith is based on that radical love, nevertheless religious dogmas add on loopholes making it possible to rationalize *not* doing unto others as you would have them do unto you—as if we could get away with it. But the secret is out—it doesn't work that way.

As far as we know, most of the world's religions were founded during the 10,000-year reign of anthropocentrism. The priests, monks, and leaders of these organized faiths were wholly immersed in the violent thinking of the times, as were their followers. Because of this, it was impossible for most of them to live by the Golden Rule, even though it was widely accepted as a human ideal. The "might makes right" way of life was in direct opposition to the Golden Rule which is why some joke that the Golden Rule really means, "Them that's got the gold makes the rules."

We can't be good so we need a scapegoat. Aware that human beings were constantly committing "sins," numerous religions came up with the idea that we could be forgiven by an all-powerful god or gods if we killed an animal or a person as a sacrifice to redeem ourselves. Sacrifices to gods were also encouraged or demanded in order to bring prosperity, good crops, and other blessings. Of course, the misguided and vicious sacrifices did bring prosperity—not to the people, but to the priests and politicians who benefitted financially from the sacrifices. This practice is so devoid of logic and empathy that it borders on the psychopathic. Nevertheless, it actually still continues today.

Horrifyingly, a Passover sacrifice of two lambs took place in 2018 near the Temple Mount, the site of the Temple that was destroyed in 70 CE where abominable sacrifices of thousands of animals took place for centuries. It was that very temple where Jesus protested the killing of the animals and the "money changers" making profits in the temple. During the 2018 Passover, "Men dressed in biblical garb danced and purified themselves, members of the priestly tribe recited the traditional blessing and two sheep were ritually slaughtered and their meat roasted…[the] gathering was not only widely advertised but also broadcast on giant screens near the Al-Aqsa Mosque, according to Channel 13."[8]

Likewise, the sacrificial practice of Kapparot continues. This ritual takes place by those who believe that killing an animal will absolve the killer of sin. Only Homo Sapiens could dream up such a strange, illogical and cruel practice. A live chicken, whose life has been one of horror, now is swung about a person's head and then killed as a scapegoat. The ritual takes place annually on the eve of Yom Kippur while the petitioner recites, *"This is my substitute, this is my vicarious offering, this is my atonement. This cock will go to its death, but I shall have a long and pleasant life of peace."*[9] Most Jewish people oppose this practice, and animal rights activists, notably Karen Davis, President of United Poultry Concerns, are working hard to end this travesty.

The words spoken at Kapparot are about as far from the Golden Rule, not to mention good sense, as one can get. It is a good example of how human beings can use religion to justify the actual opposite of the universal guiding principle of love and compassion. The Gadhimai Sacrifice that takes place every five years in Nepal to supposedly appease the Hindu Goddess Gadhimai has been a war-torn spectacle of half a million animals killed in scapegoat rituals in front of thousands of people, including children. Animal activists and many religious leaders and groups oppose it and are pleading for its termination.

While these brutal bloodbaths of innocent animals are certainly shocking, the numbers of animals sacrificed to gods and goddesses don't even come remotely close to the uncountable billions of animals sacrificed to the god of money and power in laboratories, slaughterhouses, and fishing fleets. These bloody sacrificial rituals take place, not every five years, but every single day without pause. The rivers of blood that stain the hearts and souls of humanity come from individual animals who wanted to live and be with their beloved families and friends. But those crimson rivers and piles of muscle, fat, organs, bones, and skin and the traumatized workers who are doing the killing are making the "high priests" extremely wealthy. Their "god" is good to their pocketbooks and their lust for power. However, and this is key, the beautiful, exciting truth about this is that we don't have to convince these "priests" to be nice. *All we have to do is stop buying their products and their lies.*

It is possible that Jainism, certainly the religion most dedicated to non-harm, may have preceded the animal agricultural era. Many Jains believe that their religion is tens of thousands of years old. Written documents that have survived, however, only date as far back as 9,000 years ago. Mahavira, considered the last great master, lived around 600 BCE, close to the time of the Buddha and Pythagoras. The five vows of Jainism are for nonviolence, truth, not stealing, celibacy or sexual continence, and nonattachment. These five vows sound very similar to those of Jesus and his family, as well as Pythagoras' and the Buddha's teachings. It is very possible that Jesus's ancestors knew and agreed with Pythagoras and the Jains.

Domination did creep into one sect of Jainism which claimed that a woman could not become enlightened until she reincarnated as a man. While we keep that in mind, it's important to remember that Jains have maintained hospitals for animals for hundreds of years and teach, without reservation, the value of non-harm to all living beings. Very strict Jains wear cloths over their faces to avoid accidentally inhaling insects and do not take jobs that involve animal cruelty, such as at zoos, circuses, and obviously slaughterhouses. They do not eat root vegetables, since digging them up disturbs the microbes in the soil, nor honey, since bees are abused during the stealing of their honey. For centuries, they have eaten dairy products, believing that cows generously give of their milk. However, as they discover the truth of the modern and viciously cruel dairy industry, many are giving it up entirely and becoming vegan.

So, in spite of the heavy-handed dogma of domination that has defined many religions and clouded their ability to live by the Golden Rule, the Jain faith has done better than most to live by it. If it truly is many thousands of years old, it would have developed prior to the reign of patriarchy and agriculture. That might explain how it came to develop the principles of nonviolence. As we have seen, in those prehistoric years, there is evidence of Homo Sapiens living within the partnership worldview which could have supported the Jains' five vows.

We are all an answer to Gandhi's prayer. Mahatma Gandhi was influenced by Jainism and sought to live by the vow of ahimsa. One day, while in Calcutta, he passed by the Temple of Kali. Sheep were being herded into the Temple, and "rivers of blood" were flowing out of the temple. Gandhi, in his horror and grief at the sight of the suffering lambs, began praying for "some great spirit, man or woman, fired with divine pity, who will deliver us from this heinous sin, save the lives of the innocent creatures, and purify the temple."[10] Gandhi's prayer calls out for one person that could accomplish such a task, but as it turns out, *we are all an answer to his prayer*. We are being called to purify the holy temple of earth and bring an end to the mindless sacrifices of animals to the gods of power and money.

We all know that when we hurt others, we hurt ourselves on every level—spiritually, morally, physically and mentally. Deep within our true nature, within our soul wisdom, we know that what has been done in the name of domination and power over others, is wrong, and that there must be consequences. We are living with those consequences right now, and the very survival of all beings is at stake.

> *Even in the worm that crawls in the earth*
> *there glows a divine spark. When you slaughter*
> *a creature, you slaughter God.*
> Isaac Bashevis Singer

When we forget the Golden Rule, then the opposite of that rule comes back to haunt us. Though our souls weep for what we have done, we may not hear our inner mourning. If we do unto others what we would not want done to us, then we cause similar suffering to ourselves. The violence we do to others, especially if they are defenseless against us, comes back. The universal spiritual principle that what you sow, you will also reap, is operating at full speed right now. We are all connected. The suffering of one is the suffering of all. For example:

- **Farmed Animals**: Will Tuttle points to much of what we are reaping. "We force farmed animals to live in extremely polluted and toxic environments, to breathe air made noxious by the concentrated ammonia excrement of thousands of enclosed and overcrowded animals, to live in their own waste and eat contaminated feed. We find ourselves living increasingly in our own waste as our air becomes more polluted and our water and food are increasingly contaminated."[11] Courageous animal rights activists, working undercover, have thrown open the doors that have been hiding the vile and merciless conditions in which farmed animals are living and dying. So-called "humane" farms are no better than factory farms. Clearly, we cannot destroy families, lives, homes and friends and expect our own world to be any different. We are reaping what we and our ancestors have sown this very day.

- **Animals in Laboratories**: Similarly, it is the courage of activists who have gone undercover in laboratories, physicians willing to put their careers on the line, whistleblowers in the pharmaceutical industry and many others who have revealed to us the sickening torture and killing of helpless animals in laboratories. Many drugs with terrible side-effects for human beings, including suicidal impulses and death, are now being sold to the public when responsible research has shown that a plant-based diet is usually the answer to healing disease. We are all reaping the lack of cures, the Big Pharma lies, and the destruction of human health from the seeds that have been sown in these merciless and violent laboratories.

- **Animals of the waters**: The story is the same in the seas, the rivers, and all the waters of the world. It is Homo Sapiens alone that has polluted these once thriving waters with sewage, toxic waste, plastic, lethal fishing nets, and trash. It is Homo Sapiens alone that has decimated a nearly infinite number of fishes and other innocent beings of the waters. Dead sea birds and whales are found routinely now with their bellies filled with undigestible trash. Oceana estimates that roughly forty percent of the world's marine animals are considered trash. Fishing businesses cannot use these animals to make a profit so they are literally thrown back, injured or dead, into the waters. That forty percent adds up to 63 billion pounds of animals per year. Oceana estimates that 650,000 whales, dolphins and seals were killed in nets and discarded each year during the 1990's. Each of those discarded animals and the fishes who were sold as food had lives they treasured. Each person who eats a fish has, knowingly or not, caused the deaths and trashing of many other precious animals who were thrown away as garbage for that one fish. Our species depends on the waters of the Earth for our very survival. As we sow the seeds of destruction in the waters everywhere, waters that were once pure and pristine, we reap cancer, mercury poisoning, heart disease, and other illnesses. We can stop eating fishes and polluting their waters, or we can continue to sow destruction and reap the same for us and for them.

- **Animals of the wild**, of course, are losing habitats, homes, families, and each other this very minute. Everywhere we look in our towns and cities, bulldozers are shoving over trees and filling wetlands to make way for more buildings, houses, parking lots, and highways. Dr. Seuss's *The Lorax* warned us back in the '70's. The Lorax was the guardian of the trees and the ecosystem that provided a home for the singing Swomee-Swans and others. But the Once-ler decided he could make a killing by cutting down the Truffula trees and using them to make Thneeds. Because of his cleverness and his greed, the Once-ler built quite a business by selling Thneeds to the public that loved them. But one day, *very much like today*, the Once-ler discovered that he had ignorantly cut down all the Truffula trees. The land and air were polluted and there were no animals left there. It was a tragic sight. But then he saw something strange. Our hero, the Lorax, had carved a message into a stone that read simply: "Unless." The Once-ler puzzled over that "unless" for a long time. And then one day it came to him. He had managed to save one Truffula seed. With that one seed, he could replant the forest and bring back the animals. The lesson of the story was clear back then, and now we are living with the "unless" ourselves.

We still have some seeds left.
We still have our "Unless,"
but we cannot wait any longer.

We have covered sea animals, wild creatures, farmed and lab animals. We could, of course, write an entire book detailing the horrors our species has inflicted on animals for pharmaceuticals, beauty products and fur as well as in circuses, rodeos, zoos, marine parks, aquariums, dog slaughterhouses, puppy and other pet mills, bear bile farms, horse drawn carriages, dog and horse racing, fox hunting, palm plantation monkey slaves... The list is as endless as the human imagination is of how to use and harm others. We have to stop.

Unless we apply the Golden Rule to all beings, we will continue to reap extremely un-golden results for ourselves and all others. The animals and our own spirits will continue to suffer until we bring our own actions into alignment with this most celebrated and noble of rules.

Marc Bekoff proposes a NonHuman Golden Rule. He writes, "Not using the evidence we have and not applying the Golden Rule to nonhumans is... plain and simple human exceptionalism."[12] As we rob animals of their eggs, honey, children, friends, and very lives, we rob ourselves of all that is dear to us. Our world is polluted and full of chaos, stress, broken families, hate and violence, because Homo Sapiens thought it could get away with murder—mass murder on a cataclysmic scale, forgetting that we are all sacred and interconnected, forgetting that we all share the same world and the same passion for life.

Homo Ahimsa is a species in love with all miraculous life.

> *If the sight of the blue skies fills you with joy,*
> *If a blade of grass springing up in the fields*
> *has power to move you, If the simple things*
> *in nature have a message you understand,*
> *Rejoice, for your soul is alive.*
> Eleanora Duse[13]

Our true nature, in a word, is love. Ahimsa living is love in action. We are meant to *be* love, to be creatures who love and care for all. Some say we had to go through a quasi-adolescent, self-centered, fearful period of development that led to all of our violent ways. Perhaps so. But that time is past. We cannot remain there any longer if we hope to survive as a species and heal the damage we have done. This is our big chance to become the loving, nonviolent, compassionate, peaceful creatures we have always been destined to be. *Vegan living is the Golden Rule in perfect action.* If we truly desire to live a life of nonviolence, lovingkindness, reverence and compassion for all life, that desire leads us, by definition, straight to the ahimsa life. It is a life-giving way of joy, not a life-taking existence. When we become ethically vegan, we come home to our spiritual and heart essence at last. We become Homo Ahimsa.

> *Apprehend God in all things,*
> *for God is in all things.*
> *Every single creature is full of God*
> *and is a book about God.*
> *Every creature is a word of God.*
> *If I spent enough time with the*
> *tiniest creature—even a caterpillar—*
> *I would never have to prepare a sermon.*
> *So full of God is every creature.*
> Meister Eckhart, 13th century

CHAPTER SIX

What Are the Most Effective Ahimsa Actions Each One of Us Can Take?

Though the cities start to crumble
and the towers fall around us,
The sun is slowly fading and it's
colder than the sea...the song that
I am singing is a prayer to non-believers.
Come and stand beside us, we can find a better way.
John Denver, "Rhymes and Reasons," 1969

Can we really find a better way? Many people say the world would be better off without our species in it. The Earth and the animals have suffered at human hands for centuries, and the damage is escalating so quickly, there are those who believe it's too late for us to change our ways. Deforestation; drilling; mining; polluting water, land, and air; desertification; species extinction; world hunger and poverty; war; social unrest—all these are evidence of our blindness to our soul's purpose. This is a spiritual, moral and ethical crisis, and it is happening right now.

If we refuse to change course, Yuval Noah Harari, the author of *Homo Deus,* predicts that "their [the animals'] fate may well turn out to be the greatest crime in human history. If you measure crimes by the sheer amount of pain and misery they inflict on sentient beings, this radical claim is not implausible."[1]

All this destruction can be traced, as we have discussed already, to the nearly universal and tragically twisted worldview that human beings have the right to dominate and exploit the earth, all animals, and all people who are "not one of us." This enormous misunderstanding of who we are was born out of fear. That fear has burdened us for thousands of years, because we lost our spiritual compass and our deep and very real connection to other living beings and to nature. We forgot who we were. The belief that we could only survive by violence and power over others has infiltrated even the kindest of hearts.

> *Re-examine all you have been told in school*
> *or church or in any book, and dismiss whatever*
> *insults your own soul; and your very flesh*
> *shall be a great poem…*
> Walt Whitman

This spiritual, ethical, and physical crisis we are facing demands that we leave behind this old paradigm. There can be no argument to that. The belief that we are a dominator species, with rights to destroy what we wish, is destroying us too. The good news is that people are learning, as Whitman taught, to dismiss the insults to our very souls that occur in our schools and churches, on billboards and ads, in the media and many other institutions. The damage is so obvious now. And many of us are turning within to finally come to know ourselves, question everything that we've been programmed to believe, reconnect to all life, and get busy reversing the damage we have done. But how can we do that?

We are, right now, at a crossroads, and that's a wonderful thing. It's something to be grateful for, because there are so many bells ringing now to awaken us out of this trance. Because time is of the essence, we must choose our path quickly. We can choose a new beginning that celebrates life; deprogram ourselves from cultural, political and institutional lies; transform our actions and thoughts; and reveal our true nature. Or we can ignore the damage we've done and continue on our current path of destruction to the bitter end. It really is that simple. It is absolutely up to human beings, our species alone, to save this world, not because we are superior but, on the contrary, because we are the ones who have done the damage. We have been the destroyers. No one else has done this—not bears or dogs, not alligators or cows. As Walt Kelly, creator of "Pogo," famously said on a 1970 Earth Day poster: "We have met the enemy and he is us."

Let us imagine our species entering symbolic chrysalises and emerging as new creatures. No longer voracious caterpillars, but rather graceful nectar sippers and pollinators. We were always meant to be nurturers, protectors, companions and healers of life. We were always meant to live in peace and have reverence for life and to love all others. According to the Biblical creation story we were meant to be herbivores. The imaginal cells of compassion are alive within us now, longing to reveal our beautiful wings.

However, in order to metamorphose into Ahimsa butterflies, we must regard the disintegration going on around us as a necessary part of the process. As the "towers" of the old world-view crumble and fall apart, that imaginal, magical goo is exactly what we need to liberate the new Ahimsa butterfly to bless the world.

This loving, nonviolent way of life is the opposite of the bullying, dominator path which we all know so well. Ahimsa living is the critical element if we are to save the world from destruction by Homo Sapiens' mad rush to take without giving anything in return.

Where is the hope? We desperately need to hear good news to reassure ourselves that we actually can stop the human caused Sixth Extinction, heal the waters and air, bring trees back to the decimated rainforests, get all the trash and plastic out of the oceans, end animal agriculture, and do this so all Earth's children will have a home. Let's celebrate the fact that it doesn't take much research to find a treasure box of signs that Homo Ahimsas are everywhere now, and *you all are accomplishing miracles*:

- **The number of vegans is rising steadily.** Vasile Stanescu concludes, from his search of five opinion polls from different organizations, that "there is no question that the rate of self-reported vegetarians and vegans is: a. around one in ten Americans; b. consistent; c. increasing and—most importantly; d. skewing towards higher rates (12%) for those under 50."[2]

- **The number of animal sanctuaries for animals who would have been killed, but are now rescued and safe, is increasing.** Farmed animal sanctuaries that have listed themselves on Vegan.com total 98 in the U.S in 34 states. Fifty-six sanctuaries are listed in Australia, and 39 in other countries around the world. Of course, there are many more that are not yet listed and a growing number of micro-sanctuaries as well.

- **Plant-based burgers are growing in popularity.** In 2019 Beyond Meat's vegan burgers were sold in 38,000 locations in 20 different countries. This statistic was reported—this is good news too—in a *mainstream* weekly magazine. The journal notifies its 574,000 readers that burgers made with plants "produce 90 percent fewer greenhouse gases per pound than conventional meat."[3] In an article about the "coming disruption of food," Diana Carney explains that the disruption will come from technology. She likens the food disruption that is taking place to the invention of the internal combustion machine which liberated many animals from being forced to pull plows and carriages. In a mere twenty years the U.S. virtually replaced a system based on animals to one centered on engine driven vehicles, in spite of a lack of infrastructure. She writes that "apparent shifts

in the food system—such as the current 'meat-free ma-
nia'—are driven by new technologies far more than by a
consumer spiritual awakening or a health and environmental push on the part of governments. Initially, feedback
loops hold back the new in favour of the old. Once certain
tipping points have been reached, however, such loops
begin to favour the new over the old. We then see the fa-
miliar 'S curve' of rapid adoption."[4] She has a point, no
doubt, about technology hastening this process, but I sub-
mit the "spiritual awakening" and the centuries of actions
and prayers are the reason it's happening.

- **Animals asking for help from people are opening human hearts.** A manta ray off the Ningaloo coast of
Australia saw a group of divers and swam over to them to
ask for help. She showed them the fish hooks embedded in
her skin near her eye and then waited patiently while one of
the divers removed them. Seeing this news on social media
helps undo the centuries of lies that animals are unfeeling
machines. It draws people's hearts and minds closer to understanding that animals are people too. We are all
connected in mystic ways, and helping each other is our only way ahead. Now that still and video cameras on phones
have teamed up with social media, the world is seeing a tor-
toise comforting a baby hippo, a deer bowing to a monk
who is bowing to her, divers freeing whales from fishnets, a
whale saving a woman from sharks, elephants and crows
mourning a beloved who has died, dogs and crows sledding
with their own sleds. All these years, we have missed their
senses of humor, their devotion to each other, their wisdom. But now we are ready to *see* who they are and see in
their eyes the divine that also dwells in us.

- **One hundred cities in Spain have banned bull fights.**
Eighty percent of Spaniards oppose them, and more cities

will be banning them, thanks to the unflinching, never-give-up work of activists.

- **Cows are therapists**. As the human understanding of our deep soul connection with animals grows, we find there are now not just therapy dogs and horses, but also very successful therapy cows and many other animals who, without speaking human words, are healing the most broken of hearts.

- **Bans on the use of wild animals in circuses and other good measures for animals**. California legislators made significant steps toward the right path of compassion. In 2019 the state banned the sale of fur, the trophy hunting and trapping of bobcats, the importation and sale of exotic skins, and the use of wild animals in circuses, along with other progressive measures. Many cities, as well as a long list of countries, counties and states, have banned circuses that use wild animals.

- **Consumers have the power to change the world.** While governments can be influenced by us to do the right things, we ourselves have far more power to undo Homo Sapiens' harms. Two researchers conducted a meta-analysis of 1,530 studies to try to determine, among other things, if consumers have the power to stop the destruction of ecosystems and wild animals. Clearly, governments and industries move too slowly to depend on them alone. The authors concluded that dietary change by us, "can deliver environmental benefits on a scale not achievable by producers," and called for urgent action.[5] It is we who must vote with our dollars and tell the producers that we will no longer buy their products or support their relentless destruction of ecosystems and animals' lives and families. And while it may be a shock to them at first, as the world advances in love, they will find that they too have been liberated from the chains of the old culture.

- **Many orphaned baby elephants rescued from human violence**: The David Sheldrick Wildlife Trust in Kenya overcomes evil and desperation with love every day. They rescue orphaned elephants whose mothers and aunts have been murdered by poachers and killed indirectly by people who pay high prices for ivory. One baby was spotted by a tourist who reported her to the Trust. The baby was suffering from a snare that was cutting into her neck. This baby still had her mom, but the rescuers knew it would cut more deeply as she grew. It took months to find her using helicopters and ground searches. When they finally located her and her mother, they had to move quickly. Darting the baby and keeping her anxious mother at a distance as they worked was not easy, but they succeeded in cutting the cable loose, treating the wound, and reuniting mother and child. "What a relief this must have been for both mum and her baby, and it is no small wonder why this mum was so fiercely protective having witnessed her baby's discomfort all these years, powerless to do anything about it."[6]

Hope and empowerment: These little bits of good news are a tiny fraction of all that is happening because of the many people living, working, praying, and acting from their true ahimsa nature. Reminding ourselves of all the millions of people bringing big love to the world brings us the hope and empowerment we need to believe we can make this tectonic shift in consciousness now. Let us keep close to our hearts the treasure of knowing that we are not alone in this journey we undertake. We have each other and we have Divine Intelligence and the power of love walking beside us, nudging us to take the next step, to not lose faith, to stay strong and to trust our intuition and spiritual calling. There is a collective will among us, urging us onward to create a nonviolent world and fully embody Homo Ahimsa, our true and highest nature.

When action joins forces with vision-holding, prayer, and intention, miracles happen.

> *Do not injure any living being.*
> *This is the eternal, perennial, and unalterable way of spiritual life.*
> *A weapon, howsoever powerful it may be,*
> *can always be superseded by a superior one;*
> *But no weapon can, however,*
> *be superior to nonviolence and love.*
> Jain Prayer for Peace

Through a combination of physical actions and metaphysical prayer, also known as focused thought, we greatly increase the chances that worldwide animal, Earth, and human liberation will become a reality. In addition to the physical sanctuaries for animals all over the world, Homo Ahimsa also creates sanctuaries for animals in our human hearts.

Our main job, at this point, is to create new ways of living that will free animals and heal ourselves and the Earth. While protesting, educating, and working to change laws are all vitally important and urgently needed, our most important work is creating the new partnership world of nonviolence and loving-kindness that is taking the place of the disintegrating patriarchal, anthropocentric culture in which we have been living. The steps below are a few of the loving actions we can take as we continue together to create a world of peace and harmony. Christians ask the question "What would Jesus Do?" (WWJD) as an arrow to point the way to the best action. Ironically, many Christians have not yet adopted the steps below, but that is partly because Jesus's teachings have been compromised. According to many scholars who have studied the ancient origins of Christianity, *these actions really are what Jesus would do*—and many other great spiritual teachers as well. But if WWJD is not your guiding light, here is a beautifully simple and basically identical one: what would Homo Ahimsa do (WWHAD)?

What actions can we as individuals take right now?

- **Eat plant-based**, no dead animals, no milk that belongs to baby cows and no eggs from suffering mother hens. This is *the ultimate boycott* and the most powerful physical action we can take to bring us back from the brink. In this way, we make animal agriculture obsolete and create an entirely new food system of peace, health, environmental healing, and one that can feed the entire human population on less land than is currently used to raise and feed animals killed for food. We cannot depend on governments and industries to make this happen. Politics, greed, and competition drive these players to make very destructive decisions. But one vegan, eating an all-plant diet saves approximately 1,100 gallons of water, 45 pounds of grain, 30 square feet of forested land, 20 pounds of carbon dioxide equivalent and one or more precious animals' lives every single day, according to climatevegan.org. Every single one of us on the planet can stop eating animals at our meals. In doing so, by voting with our dollars, animal agriculture will have to shut down. And it must, for it is the top cause, as I have listed previously, of pandemics and nearly every destructive force on the planet.

It sounds overwhelmingly difficult to solve these problems, but when we realize what a huge part animal agriculture plays in the destruction of life, spirit and ethics, we have the key. Eliminating that one giant Goliath of annihilation—the raising and killing of animals—we can see that, though we may not be giants, our weapon of love and eating plant-based will bring healing to all, including ourselves. It's amazing to think that we have the power to do that. We have been taught for centuries that governments rule, that change comes from the top down. But that is not true. In the partnership, ahimsa, Golden Rule model of living, we can and will create Heaven on Earth.

There is not enough time to wait for governments to do this. We have to take action ourselves. We, just us, can actually, by ourselves, avoid the annihilation cliff that animal agriculture is dragging the world toward. That giant monster industry cannot live if we no longer feed it with our dollars and our complicity. And with its bulldozers and ships and drift nets and fires and toxic waste gone, we can clean and rewild the Earth *and* rewild ourselves. With the help of nature and the animals, we can heal the wounds our species has caused. We can make this happen. Isn't that amazing?

- **Be patient and loving with ourselves** as we commit to no longer support the companies that are contributing to the ravaging of life on Earth. Even vegans, who have been attempting to do the least harm for decades, are continually finding more products that do harm. As more behind-the-scenes reports reveal the formerly hidden truth of how items are made, as well as what happens to them when they are discarded, we discover how far we have drifted away from our values.

It is fairly simple and straight-forward to give up wool, leather, fur and other articles of clothing and furniture made from the ruthless abuse and killing of animals. It is much easier now to find cruelty-free cosmetics and shampoo and soap. Hundred percent recycled toilet paper, copy paper, envelopes, and cardstock are now fairly easy to locate. But finding alternatives to our gas heat, our poison-powered electricity, fuel for our cars, and the ever-present plastic that follows us everywhere—that is very challenging. So we need to be patient with ourselves as we search for answers to these hurdles. But if you are taking part in this beautiful, miraculous and nonviolent act of simply eating only plants and holding the vision of a vegan world, then you are doing the two most important, far-reaching actions to bring peace and healing to Earth for all animals, people, and nature.

- **Meditate and do our own inner work** in order to help others awaken to their true nature as Homo Ahimsa. As people who are aware of the devastation of the Earth and the extreme suffering of animals, one of the primary spiritual tasks is to simultaneously bear witness to the ongoing atrocities and feel the ecstatic joy of our intimate connection with this beautiful world. In and around our mourning, our anger, and our doubts, we must hold fast to the absolute knowing that our vision of a paradise on Earth for all already exists in the unseen and is waiting to manifest when enough people believe. The way of truth and love is manifesting all around us. The exciting momentum is building. Remember to stop, breathe, and listen. When you take a walk in nature, even if the place has been ravaged by bulldozers or fire, you can hear the new earth singing, and asking us to sing with her, this new song of freedom and healing. And remember to celebrate silence, the gaps between thoughts where wisdom and the true self lives. Beyond ego, selfish desire, fear, and mind chatter lie peace, gratitude, and unconditional love. From there will come your true work, your own special gift to create a new, healed and peaceful world.

We need to be loving to ourselves. We have all been traumatized by our violent, fear-based cultures. We all have many layers of cultural programs to peel back and release. Nearly every system within which we have been living is tainted with old, anthropocentric ideas that we have absorbed on unconscious levels in our bodies, minds and spirits. Thankfully, we have been graced with the awareness that we can shake off these outmoded dominator rules and discover our true hearts, our true minds, and bring heaven to earth. As we sing, "Let there be peace on Earth, and let it begin with me," let us take the words to heart. For we must find our own inner peace, our own inner ahimsa, and fall in love with who we really are, if we are to bring this high consciousness to the world. Rumi said, "The wound is the place where the light enters you." Whatever calls to you to help you heal and find this peace within, take time to do that in your meditations. And know this—that, as you cleanse your body from the violence of eating flesh, eggs, and milk, your spirit will also be cleansed in many ways.

One of the most powerful practices we can do for ourselves and the world is gratitude. By practicing deep gratitude, fear cannot grip us. In gratitude, we celebrate life. In gratitude, we leave the dying matrix behind, and fear can no longer slow our awakening consciousness. When we are aligned with love and gratitude, our vibration synchronizes with all who are awakening now.

When we first awaken to the horrors committed by humanity to nature, animals, and people, we are halfway to joy. That may sound strange, but it happens because we have gone beyond our own egos and survival instincts and now feel true compassion and connection with others. As we enter this phase of our higher nature, we begin to understand that we are here to live in such a secure state of inner peace and joy that we are well equipped to help bring about a world of peace and joy for all others.

- **Join with other animal lightworkers**. Find communities that are dedicated to creating a kind, gentle world for all life. Whether online or in-person, we need each other for encouragement, as well as to work together to share this consciousness raising, Homo-Ahimsa-waking news. Many activist groups in cities and small towns chalk sidewalks, march, hold vigils for and offer water to thirsty animals being taken to slaughter, show videos on the street of what really happens to animals (such as Cube of Truth actions), celebrate and educate with VegFests (popping up everywhere!), have potlucks and food demos, show films to small and large audiences, host speakers, host podcasts and zoom meetings—the list is endless. Thanks to the internet and the growing numbers of lightworkers, it is easier than ever to find kindred spirits.

> *You may say I'm a dreamer,*
> *but I'm not the only one.*
> John Lennon

- **Plant lots of seeds.** Consciousness liberators are a lot like dandelions. Some people would rather we not appear in their lawns even though our bright yellow blossoms are quite beautiful. They try to pull us up by the roots or spray us with herbicides of all kinds, but, somehow, we always manage to pop back up cheerily and then overnight turn into the loveliest puffballs, full of hundreds of seeds. All we need is a little wind and there go our seeds flying about like tiny birds. That's why the number of activists increases every day. The dandelion-hearted ones have planted a lot of seeds with both prayers and actions. These seeds of love are blowing everywhere and landing on fertile soil. We pray for the rain of lovingkindness and the sunshine of universal love to nurture these seeds. We pray for strength and courage and wisdom so that we may do our part, each one of us, to bring true joy and love to the world and to all beings.

- **Pray and visualize.** We save what we love. Let us love and visualize this planet and all those who live here into a paradise of peace. Carl Jung taught that "what you resist persists." That is why it is vitally important and powerful to create the new, rather than only wage war against the old. We are willing the seemingly impossible into existence, just as slavery abolitionists, peace workers and those who have worked for human and animal rights have done over the centuries. The paradigm shifts that we see so far blazed into reality because activists carried their dreams into the light and because God, or Universal Love, is always moving and dancing with every leap in human consciousness, no matter how tiny that leap might be.

Gandhi said, "When I despair, I remember that all through history the way of truth and love have always won... Think of it—always." Holding the vision of a world in which no people or animals are exploited by human beings helps to bring that into reality. The more people who hold that intention, see it in their minds, imagine it, and feel the joy of it, the more power is generated to bring it into the tangible, visible world. Love is the most powerful force that exists in the universe. All we need to do is get in synch with it. When we really think about it, vegan nonviolent living is the ultimate spirituality, the Golden Rule in action, and the highest form of consciousness in which we realize the sacredness of ourselves and all others. It is the practice of unconditional, selfless love from which comes the healing of the world.

We are not trying to destroy the dominator paradigm. It is dying on its own, and it is being replaced with something beautiful. If we ask almost any person if they would hurt an animal on purpose, nearly all will say an emphatic "no." And yet, as we know, in our current cultures, well-meaning, kind-hearted people hurt animals continually every single day. But they don't want to. They are, heart and soul, already vegan, already in touch with their ascended nature. Just a few more steps! As activists educate, Divine Love accelerates our trajectory to ascension. As patriarchy burns up in its own firestorms around the world, we are kneeling in the ashes, cradling the wounded in our arms, and blessing the soft earth. The dream, the vision of a healed and revealed world holds steady.

Someday, after we have mastered the winds,
the waves, the tides, and gravity, we shall
harness for God the energies of love.
Then, for the second time in the history
of the world, [people] will have discovered fire.
Teilhard de Chardin

- **Assist on the ground with this epic transition.** If we are able, we can rescue animals and get them to homes and sanctuaries. There is also much to be done to help animal agriculture workers transition. While we are making animal agriculture irrelevant and replacing it with plant-based food so that everyone can be fed, we do need to plan for what will happen to the farmed animals themselves and those who have made their livelihoods in this grisly business. As was mentioned earlier, the number of animal sanctuaries is growing, as more animals are rescued from slaughter, and, as ranchers and farmers decide they can no longer bear the expense or, for some, the heartache of killing animals. Renee King-Sonnen, director of Rowdy Girl Sanctuary, and her husband Tommy, converted their cattle ranch into a farmed animal sanctuary and now help other ranchers and animal farmers make a similar transition. Their Rancher Advocacy Program (RAP) helps people convert their businesses away from killing animals to making a living by growing vegetables, mushrooms, nut trees, and other plant-based undertakings that can heal the Earth and stop animal suffering.

They help ranchers whose hearts have begun to hear the cries of the animals they have been sending to slaughter. In these days of rapid ethical and spiritual transformation, many want to stop being a part of the heart-breaking death marches for the animals they have raised. The Rancher Advocacy Program helps them find alternative ways to make a living and to feel the joy of saving lives, and "…make a difference in the world, and be prosperous in our growing climate of plant-based food options and other innovative solutions to animal agriculture and the health and longevity of the earth."[7]

Some of our actions could include volunteering at sanctuaries, rescuing animals from slaughter, and helping farmers, slaughterhouse workers and others find meaningful work that is healing for them and for the world. Many of these people don't know or cannot even imagine that there is another way for them to make a living. They need our help and compassion, just as the animals do.

- **Listen to the animals and talk to them**. Chief Dan George advises us to talk to animals. "If you do, they will talk back to you. But if you don't talk to the animals, they won't talk back to you, then you won't understand, and when you don't understand you will fear, and when you fear you will destroy the animals, and if you destroy the animals, you will destroy yourself." We are their beloveds, and they are waiting for us to see them as *our* beloveds.

Visiting a sanctuary, where animals are safe after being rescued from slaughter or enslavement, is a wonderful way to heal our hearts and listen to the animals. Taking a friend or family member to visit a sanctuary is a powerful way to help them understand that all animals are individuals with loves and lives of their own.

I live in a rural area where many people let their dogs run free. It is great fun for the dogs but not so fun for the wilderness animals who fear them. One day I heard a commotion behind the house and saw three dogs chasing a baby deer whom they had just found sleeping in the tall grass. I didn't know I could run so fast, but I caught up with them just in time. They had the baby cornered and terrified in the creek bed. I grabbed the baby who was bleeding from a bite and ran to the house with him in my arms. As I got to the house, I saw the mama deer watching me. I called to her, "I will help your baby and bring him back to you," a promise I prayed I could keep.

I drove the injured baby to our wildlife rehabilitation center for care. They gently cleaned, stitched and dressed the wound and thought they would need to keep him overnight. However, as I was leaving, they decided his best chance for healing would be for me to get him back to his mother right away. So off we went, the slightly groggy fawn and I, back to Mama. When we arrived at my house, it was growing dark. I looked past the garage to the edge of the forest. I could barely see her, but there she was. My heart rejoiced when I saw her standing there, faithfully waiting for the return of her baby. I had him in my arms, carrying him toward her, when suddenly he spotted her and his little legs started running before I could even place him on the ground. And off they ran together into the forest. I believe to this day that his mother heard my words and trusted me to bring her child back safely to her. Yes, we do need to talk to the animals. To do so is to acknowledge their dignity, sovereignty, and their intelligence. More importantly, we must listen to them for they can teach us much of what we desperately need to know at this critical time in our transformation.

- **Go organic.** Support regenerative, organic, veganic agriculture. Not all of us can grow our own food, but we can certainly support local growers and their plant-based products that are grown at least organically, and hopefully veganically, when we purchase food. As with so many other far-reaching actions of ahimsa living, by eating organic and veganic food, we are making sure we are not complicit in the use of herbicides, pesticides, slaughterhouse waste-laden fertilizers, chemicals and other practices. We help bring to an end the deaths of bees, butterflies, insects, birds, and wilderness animals, whose homes have been turned into barren, poisonous, monocrop fields, when we support agriculture that heals the Earth, promotes health, and saves animal lives.

- **Connect with activists for many causes, people of faith and spiritual leaders.** We *all* share a vision of a better world, free of violence, environmental degradation and war. The connections and overlaps among us, from the distant past through to today, create a beautiful tapestry. As more threads are woven into it, we begin to realize that we are all working on different aspects of the same vision. We all have something radiant to add as we weave together. As the old, unworkable world disintegrates around us, our imaginal cells are taking the new butterfly, Homo Ahimsa form. Together, with all these weavers, we are making it clear to the world that Homo Sapiens has done enough damage, and Homo Ahimsa is here now to create a vegan, nonviolent world of joy, peace, liberation, abundance, and love for all beings.

Those are just a few of the many steps we Homo Ahimsas are and will be taking. You have probably thought of many more. There is so much to do. But please remember that you are not alone in this massive birthing of ourselves as gentle partners in this astonishingly beautiful world. In our meditations and prayers, let us find what is ours to do each day, let us know that others are doing their own special work along with us and may we always be mindful that Divine Love is holding our hands every step of the way. In that way, we can be at peace in our work, rather than feeling that we have to do it all by ourselves. We are definitely not alone, and we cannot fail, because we are aligned with Love.

Add More Great Ideas Here:

CHAPTER SEVEN

The Power of *Seeing* Homo Ahimsa's Partnership Paradise of Peace and Freedom for All Earthlings

We have the heart to do this. The World Resources Institute and many other entities recognize that we have to change our habits of over-consumption, but they doubt that people will do that. They believe that most people just hope that industry and government will fix the problems. They are severely underestimating the power of each one of us. We not only know that industry and government cannot solve these problems in time, but that the heart for the healing *is in individual people and grass roots groups*. As we envision a healed, nonviolent and loving world, we are trusting that the ahimsa nature, that lives and breathes within each human being alive today, will arise, mature and shine forth.

One of our most important jobs is to *see* the stunning beauty of Homo Ahimsa's world. It's vital that we imagine and visualize the newly healed world. It's been documented that athletes who visualize themselves getting better at their sport can improve their performance more than those who do not use visualization. By holding positive images in the mind and feeling the thrill of getting better, the brain is convinced that the improved performance is real, and the rest of the body accepts the new reality and follows through. Action and vision go hand in hand to bring our dreams into the physical realm.

Jim Carrey tells his story of manifesting success on several online videos. Even though he was poor and not yet a famous actor, he had a clear vision of himself being successful and told himself repeatedly what others would eventually say about his talent, as if it was them talking to him in the present moment. He studied self-help books and learned some of the secrets of manifestation. Early in this process, Carrey wrote himself a check for ten million dollars and postdated it for several years ahead. By the time the check's date became current, he had been paid that much for his work in TV and films.

A short version of the manifestation process includes imagining that you have already reached your goal. It's critical to involve all the senses—hearing, taste, smell, seeing and touch—to fully experience and celebrate the achievement. Another important step is to live as if you have already accomplished the goal. Students of this process often create a dream board with pictures and words that show what it is they are manifesting. Gazing at this board often during the day helps us say "yes!" to this true way that is unfolding.

We can use these manifestation steps to help create a compassionate world of lovingkindness. Many people have found they have reached seemingly impossible personal goals, partly because of visualizing themselves already successful. We can use the same techniques to create a vegan, nonviolent, ahimsa world. And as millions of us take part in this mind shift, we can actually fill the noosphere, or field of mind, as de Chardin called it, with this vision. As the noosphere fills with beauty and kindness, the collective consciousness of Homo Sapiens will be powerfully inspired to bring about the metamorphosis of our species. Of course, we will continue to educate and take actions on the physical plane, just as the visualizing basketball player continues to shoot hoops. But this prayerful work helps in mystical and cosmic ways to elevate consciousness on the spiritual, metaphysical plane and hastens the advent of Homo Ahimsa.

It seems highly likely that most human beings have at least an unconscious longing for a garden of Eden or paradise on Earth. It is as if there is a shared memory that a place of peace once existed long ago. The Bible and many other texts speak of such a heavenly home on Earth where animals and people lived together in sacred friendship. But even if it didn't exist in the physical realm, the fact remains that the vast majority of people on the planet wish for such a place and wonder why we are so far away from it. We see the remnants of that dream every year in December when the words "Peace on Earth" seem to be everywhere. I believe that the seeds of that dream are in every human heart, perhaps, deeply hidden, but there, nevertheless, waiting to be tended and watered and loved.

But how can we believe in paradise in the midst of so much misery? It's not so easy when we find ourselves immersed in the chaotic world of violence and cruelty in which we currently live. Unless we refuse to listen to the news, watch tv, or talk with other people, we cannot help but be bombarded by daily doses of serial killers, undercover revelations of animal torture and killing, sex slavery, priests and scout leaders sexually molesting children, starvation, wars—I know, it's enough to break us. Our empathy for all those who are suffering can put us into a lasting state of dread and mourning. So, we walk a razor's edge.

Somerset Maugham's 1944 book, *The Razor's Edge*, (followed by a film of the same name), tells the story of Larry, a World War I soldier. He has returned from the war psychologically unable and unwilling to rejoin his well-to-do friends and live the way he did before his war experience. It seems to him that they are living lives without much meaning. He embarks on a spiritual journey, a dark night of the soul, and travels to India. There, he meets a spiritual teacher who guides him in his search for inner light and peace. Larry reaches a state of pure joy when he experiences his oneness with God. At that point, although Larry wants to stay with his teacher, the holy man explains that Larry must return home. But the teacher assures him that, in spite of all the tragedy that he will witness back in the world, he will always carry with him the pure knowledge of the illuminated beauty of God which dwells in all beings, all people. Wherever he goes, whatever he sees, his joy and love for all will be with him and he will be able to be of profound service to others.

How can we apply this to our own lives? It is that very awareness of and gratitude for the ecstatic beauty of life that moves our spirits so profoundly. It is that wisdom and joy that causes us to want to bring out that love and that beauty into the world to bless everyone and to stop the violence and the suffering. Because of Larry's enlightenment experience, he could navigate more gracefully within the challenging world he found back home, while simultaneously holding onto the vision of what was true and beautiful behind, within and beyond the ugliness. That's Homo Ahimsa.

All who have seen, felt, and heard the brilliance of pigs; the gentleness of cows; the faithfulness of dogs; the glory of trees and flowers; and the magical movement of fishes and birds have touched the astonishing divine that lives and breathes in every earthling and the stones and the soil as well.

> By means of all created things—without exception,
> the Divine assails us, penetrates us, molds us.
> Pierre Teilhard De Chardin

As an example of how to walk this razor's edge, let's say we are working to stop circuses from being allowed to use our animal cousins in their acts. In order to be effective, we have to expose ourselves to the horrors that the animals endure. How do we survive seeing that abominable cruelty? We do it with faith that we will succeed. We check and see that hundreds of cities, some states and even countries have banned animal circuses. Our confidence gains traction as we see that others have succeeded.

And we do it while visualizing a world in which there simply are no circuses that use, torture and kill animals.

Holding that vision in our hearts, minds, and spirits causes our ahimsa nature to grow and mature. It also gives us the strength to stay with the mission, because we can see the light ahead, the stunning beauty of a world in which it would be unthinkable to force an elephant to stand on a tiny stool and spend her life in chains. This world that we live in now is distorted and perverted by the fears of human beings. It is an appearance that will fall away as we persist in knowing and seeing the only infinite and real way of living—which is to live together in a constant state of wonder, gratitude, and communion with all of life.

We are the vision keepers, and we do not dream this alone. The paradise, where wild horses run and all beings are free, already exists on the spiritual plane. The more we believe that and see that and live that, the sooner we will bring it forth onto the material plane. We all have been given the gift of imagining and yearning for this home where not just a few of us, *but all people*, have reverence for life. The outmoded human supremacy idea, that all life is here for the human species to use however it wants, has completely disintegrated and is just a distant memory. It is of no use to anyone. Instead we find a new paradigm of compassion and communion with all life.

Isn't it wonderful that we do not carry this vision alone? The animals dream with us—all the wild horses; all the animal prisoners in labs; the animals suffering in farms; the wild animals being trapped, poisoned, and rounded up; the sea creatures caught and dying in nets; the trees and flowers—all *our relations dream with us.*

And Divine Love, the Spirit of Compassion, dreams with us as well. We envision together this freedom and *see* together the Spirit of Love made visible. We do not dream this alone.

How is it we can see what so many people don't see? How did our spirits awaken to this cosmic vision? The spirits of all people know this picture of peace, yet so few actually believe it can be manifested. Somehow our hearts and our spirits just know. It lives in us and moves us to action. It is a precious gift indeed. The animals, all of nature and we are the vision keepers. We live it and breathe it with the animals and the Earth. Our spirits run with the animals, always toward home, toward the peaceable kingdom, with courage and boldness, holding onto the dream.

> *Whatever you can do or dream you can,*
> *begin it. Boldness has genius,*
> *power and magic in it.*
> Goethe

Whatever we do, no matter how discouraged we may get, no matter how hopeless our work may seem at times, let us hold the vision of all earthlings living free. Let us hold fast to this bold dream of the coming peaceable kingdom for all life here on earth.

> *The time will come when men such as I*
> *will look upon the murder of animals*
> *as they now look on the murder of men.*
> Leonardo da Vinci

Sailesh Rao envisions this "Greatest Transformation in Human History," as a time in which we will metamorphose from:

- "Becoming extinct to Becoming Transformed"
- "Normalized Violence to Normalized Nonviolence"
- "Predator Species to Caretaker Species"
- "Homo Sapiens to Homo Ahimsa"[1]

So what exactly does Homo Ahimsa's vegan world of equality, service, radiant health, regeneration, love, compassion, abundance, and nonviolence to all look like? As we go through this list, one by one, please picture these in your mind, in vivid color and with a feeling of great joy and celebration. Use all your senses to embrace these. In your imagination, touch, taste, hear, see and smell this world. Perhaps, create a dream board with pictures of what some of these might look like. *Know,* deep in your soul, that these things are coming into manifestation now:

- All human beings live by vegan values of nonviolence and non-harm and have become Homo Ahimsa.
- All people have learned who they really are and have found that they love themselves and every other being.
- All restaurants, hospitals, schools, places of worship, and companies serve only plant-based meals and have zero waste. It is unthinkable to confine or kill an animal for food or for any other reason.
- All zoos have been transformed into sanctuaries for those animals who cannot be released to the wild and others who need care. For those who can be set free, the doors to their cages are open at last.
- All marine parks have released all those who can survive in the sea and have transformed into sacred sanctuaries and hospitals for those who cannot.
- Circuses entertain audiences with only human artists and athletes. Animals are never hurt or used for any kind of entertainment.
- Laboratories, where innocent animals once suffered for drugs, cosmetics, cleaning products, and for teaching anatomy and medical procedures, no longer exist. The buildings have been spiritually cleansed and are used as offices, apartments or greenhouses. The cages and torture implements have been recycled into pieces of art or functional tools.
- All animals are now free from human violence and exploitation. Those who have not become extinct are able to find the habitats and food that they need, do their part in re-

balancing ecosystems, and have families that will be left unmolested by Homo Ahimsa.

- There are no "No Hunting" signs, because no one would think of hunting and killing an animal.

- Musicians are often seen playing instruments and singing with cows and whales and prairie dogs.

- The fields of the Earth that were used to confine animals and grow animal feed, as well as trap and poison wild animals, have been restored to their rightful residents, those who lived there before they were expelled or killed. The grasses, flowers, herbs and trees there are cleansing themselves of the toxic herbicides and pesticides and celebrating. Beneath the ground, the vast network of roots and fungi are communicating again with each other, nourishing the soil and the new baby plants and trees.

- The fields, greenhouses and forests where food for people and animal companions is grown are clean and beautiful, producing healthy, organic, veganic food. The nearly one billion, formerly hungry people now have plenty to eat. World hunger is a thing of the past.

- The streams and rivers of the Earth are clear and clean and run joyfully into the oceans which are now free of all the chemicals, plastic and trash that Homo Sapiens once dumped there so thoughtlessly.

- Many hospitals are no longer needed, due to the healing properties of plant-based food. Those that remain teach holistic healing and lifestyle medicine.

- Slaughterhouses have become greenhouses and have been cleansed spiritually and physically of the tragedies that occurred there. Truck trailers that once carried terrified animals to slaughter have been cleansed and converted into many kinds of shelters.

- Slaughterhouse workers, ranchers, meat packers, circus and aquarium animal trainers, commercial fishermen, and animal laboratory workers have no desire to work in their former industries. They are healing from the post-traumatic stress of working those jobs and have found work that nourishes and heals them.

- People everywhere feel more joy and compassion than they have ever felt before. Pythagoras said, "as long as men massacre animals, they will kill each other. Indeed, he who sows the seeds of murder and pain cannot reap joy and love." Will Tuttle agrees, saying, "The price we pay for this [eating animal flesh and secretions] is incalculable and includes, among other things, the dulling of our innate intelligence and compassion and a consequent loss of peace, freedom, and joy." But now that everyone is living the vegan life and has become Homo Ahimsa, the joy and love of life with which we were born comes back to everyone and gives us cause to celebrate each moment here on Earth.

- Governments and hierarchical systems, as we have known them, do not exist. Decisions are made, and work and play are accomplished through mutual respect and egalitarian partnership processes.

- A profit and growth driven economy is a thing of the past. Businesses thrive, not on perpetual growth at the expense of nature, animals and people, but on the partnership model of whatever helps everyone thrive.

- The human population has leveled off. Women around the world have become liberated and educated. As a species we are in touch on a biological level, as other animals are, with balancing our desire for children with the available food supply and our intimate knowledge of the ecosystems around us.

- Addictions, murders, sex trafficking, spousal abuse, pornography, child slavery, rape and other tragic human behaviors are dim memories. Homo Ahimsa is in love with life, with self, with all glorious earthlings and cannot imagine doing any of those atrocities.

- Indigenous people who wish to remain isolated and forage for their own food find that their homes, that had been invaded by industry, belong to them again. They find peace and safety at last. As their own places of peace regenerate, they have access to good plant food, clean air and pure water once again.

- There are "Never Again" sacred memorials all over the world for animals who have been tortured and killed by people. Some are constructed out of farm, lab, hunting, and other torture implements and turned into art.

- Homo Ahimsa is nonviolent and, therefore, has no need for a military, and, of course, wars are irrelevant and nonexistent. Children who are born into the ahimsa world are baffled by the history of war.

- Memorials abound also for the many human cultures that have suffered under corrupt governments as slaves, soldiers, and victims of war and genocide.

- Non-breeding sanctuaries take care of all the farmed animals who long ago endured hell on earth from Homo Sapiens. Somehow, in their sacred wisdom, they have forgiven us, and we now live together in mutual admiration and gratitude.

- The animals no longer "flee from the sight of us." They are no longer afraid of us. Just as squirrels play with young turkeys in the woods, they now play with us too. (This is one of my favorites.)

- People of all faiths have a new, intimate connection with all life and are able to communicate with plants and animals and fungi. No one can feel any remnants of speciesism or any other 'isms, because now we are Homo Ahimsa, connected and in love with all life.

- There are no global "pandemics" and the loss of individual freedom associated with them, because there is no more animal agriculture and no more domination of people by hierarchical systems. Those systems are irrelevant now, because Homo Ahimsa is free and empowered by love.

If we surrendered to earth's intelligence,
we could rise up rooted as trees.
Rumi

Please take a little time here to breathe in the joyful feeling of these beautiful thoughts and visions. As you think of more, please add your visions below.

Your Awesome Ahimsa Ideas

If you have built castles in the air,
your work will not be lost;
that is where they should be.
Now put the foundations under them.
Henry David Thoreau

Even though this vision exercise might feel a little pie-in-the-sky, it's not. This is some of the most important work we have to do. It's difficult, I know. Our days are filled with the exact opposite appearance in the outer world. Every day brings more news of atrocities toward people and animals, desecration of the Earth, diseases, pandemics, mass shootings, desperate people acting out of rage and hatred, abandoned children and animals, but all that is exactly why this work is so important. It is, ironically, the desperation of the times that is opening the door to this new way of living. As we discussed in chapter one, we are running out of time. We cannot keep living as destroyers or we will not be able to remain a species on this planet, and many others will disappear with us. As dire as that sounds, it is really the very push we need to shock and jolt us all into action. We have needed this loudly ringing alarm for a long time. And here it is. That is something to celebrate. This is our big chance, the window in time to do this glorious thing.

The future for my precious children and grandchildren and yours, and everyone else's too, depends on what path we choose, what vision we hold, and what we do from here. It is we, who have been struck with wonder and awe by flowers and butterflies, who see the dangers ahead. Our awakened souls call us to take action. We are changing the worldview of human supremacy to one of communion with all life, as it was always meant to be. We are bringing heaven to earth at long last.

May all people around the world be filled with the sudden recognition that every animal is an individual with hopes and dreams of their own. And in that sudden clarity, may the wars against animals finally end. We will pray this prayer, and we will take peaceful action to bring this wisdom and love into every human heart. We give thanks for all the progress that has been made toward ending the wars against animals and nature and people. With each bit of good news, we rejoice.

We give thanks for this mission of ours, that somehow by some miracle, we have been blessed with this precious connection to all life. We give thanks for all activists, working so hard and refusing to lose hope. Sometimes it seems impossible, but when we look at how far consciousness has risen and how compassion has encircled the Earth for all beings, we know these crimes, these wars, must come to an end. Nearly all people say they love animals. That love is a spark of hope. May those sparks become flames of love that bring freedom and peace to all sacred life. May Divine Wisdom, the animals' grace, and our true hearts guide us toward ahimsa, lovingkindness, peace, and liberation for all.

Together let us reveal ourselves as

Homo Ahimsa,

and heal the wounds humanity has caused
to nature, each other, and the animals.
We see all of us awakening to our true
radiance and to our higher consciousness.
We see us all becoming bringers of light
and love. We see all beings full of
joy and free. We see:

Compassion encircling the Earth
for all beings everywhere.

RESOURCES

It wasn't that long ago that there were only three or four vegan cookbooks. In just a few decades, we now have thousands. And there are books, magazines, websites, films, organizations of all sizes, and on-the-ground work of all kinds. Lightworkers around the world share information, strategies, photos, recipes, events, and creative ways to bring about a nonviolent world of partnership for all beings. But rather than listing all of them and their awesomeness, I decided to limit this list to a few of the resources in which I am directly involved. May they benefit you and your work in miraculous ways.

AllCreatures.org

AllCreatures.org was founded by Reverend Frank and Mary Hoffman. It is a vast resource for spiritual and animal liberation information. On the website, you can sign up for the excellent weekly newsletter to receive breaking news, a calendar of events, and weekly sermons from vegan minister, Reverend Frank. If you are looking for a **vegan minister near you**, a vegan church or a vegan-friendly church, Allcreatures.org/church/churchdi lists them.

A Prayer for Compassion

A Prayer for Compassion is a film by Thomas Jackson. It "…asks the question, 'Can compassion grow to include all beings? Can people who identify as religious or spiritual come to embrace the call to include all human and nonhuman beings in our circle of respect and caring and love?'" The film contains interviews of many spiritual leaders of different faiths who affirm that mercy, nonviolence and love are our highest callings. The film is a wonderful way to get a discussion started with pre-vegans and to help people understand ahimsa principles. Following the showing of the film, you can host a discussion and help interested people form **Compassionate Living Circles** and take The **Compassionate Living Challenge**. The Circles provide a structure to form a study group at a place of worship or someone's home for those who have been inspired by the film. They provide a way to support new and aspiring vegans on an ongoing basis, and if formed within a place of worship, the Circle can help establish vegan practices there. The film trailer, information on how to show it and host a discussion after the film, Thomas's Challenge and Four Pillars of Well Being, how to form a Compassionate Living Circle and excellent links to other films and websites can be found at Aprayerforcompassion.com.

Circle of Compassion and
Worldwide Prayer Circle for Animals

The Circle of Compassion founded by me, Judy Carman, and Will and Madeleine Tuttle hosts: the Worldwide Prayer Circle for Animals, the daily noon prayer translated into many languages, flyers to hand out, articles, many prayers for animals, and a way to sign up to receive Will's Daily Inspiration, and Judy's Prayer for the Week. Because prayer gains power and effectiveness when our very lives are reflections of our prayers, we encourage prayer partners to adopt a nonviolent, vegan lifestyle. The spiritual connection between us and our animal cousins grows out of the understanding that we are all expressions of an infinite loving Presence, and as we acknowledge this interconnectedness and live in harmony with it, our very lives become prayers of compassion and healing.

We are working together in one spirit with the animals to create the most massive paradigm shift ever known. We are praying and envisioning together the dawning of a new humanity—one that finally and truly understands that all life is sacred and interconnected. Please join the Prayer Circle for Animals Facebook group to post prayer requests for animals and the raising of human consciousness. Circleofcompassion.org.

And please repeat with us the global visionary prayer each day at noon:

Compassion Encircles the Earth
for All Beings Everywhere.

Climate Healers and Prevent Year Zero

Climate Healers and Prevent Year Zero were founded by Sailesh Rao to help us navigate from a "Predator species, Homo Sapiens, to a Caretaker Species, Homo Ahimsa." Members have formed subgroups, within a Basecamp forum, that address various systems, such as the economy, the environment, politics and governance, and spirituality. These groups are crafting ways to re-form each system in order to create **a Vegan World by 2026,** i.e. year zero, the year by which there may no longer be any wild vertebrates left living if we do not change our destructive ways. This busy think tank also contains groups dedicated to sharing metamorphosizing films, such as "A Prayer for Compassion." On the website, you'll find blogs by Sailesh, videos, films, and books, and other resources. Climatehealers.org

Compassionate Spirit

Compassionate Spirit lists books by Kate Lawrence and Keith Akers, including her *Practical Peacemaker* and his *The Lost Religion of Jesus: Simple Living and Nonviolence in Early Christianity* and articles to guide us toward ahimsa simple living, peace, and veganism. Compassionatespirit.com.

Interfaith Vegan Coalition

Interfaith Vegan Coalition (IVC), sponsored by In Defense of Animals was founded by Lisa Levinson, myself (Judy Carman) and Thomas Jackson. Its purpose is to help activists and spiritual leaders bring vegan values to their faith and ethical communities. The guiding ideals of most traditions are identical to the Golden Rule, including nonviolence, and lovingkindness. At IVC you'll find Advocacy Kits, specific to different religions, that can help leaders practice and expand these ideals to include all sacred life, including our animal cousins. There are kits for Christian, Islam, Judaism, Zoroastrian, Sikh, Hindu, Quaker, Unity, Buddhist, Catholic, Pagan, and Jain faiths so far, and more will be added. There is also a General Kit with ideas that would apply to any faith or ethical tradition. Each kit contains famous spiritual teachers' thoughts on nonviolence and not eating animals, books, films, articles, and many other useful resources to help you with introducing vegan values. Because this is a coalition, other like-spirited groups are also members, such as **Dharma Voices for Animals, Christian Vegetarian Association, and Jewish Veg**. All these groups have many useful resources as well, and links to them can be found at IVC. Idausa.org/campaign/sustainable-activism/interfaith-vegan-coalition.

Main Street Vegan

Main Street Vegan is Victoria Moran's website where you can listen to podcasts in which she interviews vegan leaders with great ideas for our transformation. You can also find her insightful blogs and enroll in her Main Street Vegan Academy for Life Style Coaches. Victoria is also one of the producers of *A Prayer for Compassion* and author of many books, including *Main Street Vegan, The Love-Powered Diet, and the Good Karma Diet*. Mainstreetvegan.net.

Prayers and Animal Prayer Flags

This is my (Judy's) website. Here you can find my blogs, some prayers to use, a set of quotes that show we cannot have world peace as long as we eat animals, and links to my other books, ***Peace to All Beings****: Veggie Soup for the Chicken's Soul* and my book (with Tina Volpe), *The Missing Peace: The Hidden Power of Our Kinship with Animals.* You will also see the Animal Prayer Flag project, and a slide show of flags around the world, accompanied by Daniel Redwood's beautiful song, "With Us, Not For Us." Hundreds of prayer flags for animals are now flying around the world to help make sure our prayers are filling the energy field of the Earth with visions of a world in which all beings are free to live in joy and peace. There is also a useful flyer on this website entitled, "**Ten Steps**: Bring Vegan Values of compassion, nonviolence and justice to your place of worship." This is produced by the Interfaith Vegan Coalition and can be ordered there or you can make copies from my website. Under "Music for the Animals," you can hear more of Daniel Redwood's songs, and "Maybe JC Was a Vegetarian" by Paul Seymour. Peacetoall-beings.com.

Spiritual Forum

Spiritual Forum. If you have ever longed to hear a vegan minister speak, you can check out these online gatherings led by **vegan Unity minister** Reverend Carol Saunders. She might also be able to officiate as a visiting minister to bring a message of love for all beings to your church. Her online talks and blogs are uplifting and help us gain the spiritual tools we need to do this transformational work. TheSpiritualForum.org.

Sustainable Activism

The Sustainable Activism Campaign of In Defense of Animals, directed by Lisa Levinson "helps people who help animals deal with compassion fatigue, burnout, and secondary trauma caused by the tragedy-filled nature of their noble work. We support animal activists by providing emotional and spiritual resources including a support line, an online support group, and monthly webinars with experts in the field of animal protection and activist self-care." Idausa.org/sustainableactivism.

Vegan Spirituality

Vegan Spirituality was founded by Lisa Levinson, because she believed there were many people who are vegan for spiritual or ethical reasons, so that, for them veganism is a spiritual path. She asks, "Is compassion for all living beings fundamental to your spiritual beliefs? You can honor your vegan ethics and nurture your spiritual self by joining our Vegan Spirituality Community, which is part of a larger movement of spiritual vegans who adopt this way of life to foster world peace, practice nonviolence, and end the suffering of nonhuman animals. Our vision is to liberate animals, raise the consciousness of human beings, and create community based on compassion for all sentient beings. We offer spiritual support to animal activists working to free animals from human exploitation." VS helps people start their own local groups, and it hosts retreats and online gatherings. Every other month, Lisa and I interview vegan spiritual leaders in an online gathering. These are archived. Idausa.org/vegan-spirituality.

Vegetarian Friends

Vegetarian Friends publishes the spiritually uplifting. and always educational, monthly "Peaceable Table." VF "is dedicated to providing inspiration and support for Quakers and other people of faith in the practice of love for animals and a vegetarian diet." The journal is a project of the Quaker Animal Kinship (QUAK) and is edited by Gracia Fay Ellwood, author of *Taking the Adventure: Faith and our Kinship with Animals.* The website has many excellent links, and you can access all the past journals there as well. Gracia Fay's animal activist pioneer articles are especially fascinating and inspiring. Vegetarianfriends.net.

World Peace Diet headquarters

The World Peace Diet book, written by Will Tuttle, Ph.D., "…offers a set of universal principles for all people of conscience, from any religious tradition, that show how we as a species can move our consciousness forward…" On this website, you can see Dr. Tuttle's speaking itinerary, his other books, music and essays, Madeleine Tuttle's visionary animal liberation art, and how to become a World Peace Diet Facilitator. Worldpeacediet.com

PRAYERS

Be the one who, when you walk in,
Blessing shifts to the one who needs it most.
Even if you've not been fed, Be bread.
Jelaladdin Rumi

We are eternal consciousness. We are spiritual beings, and, while we are currently having a physical experience, we are daily discovering that our soul's purpose is to bring more love to the world and, indeed, to seize this "dark night" opportunity to help usher in the glorious and long awaited transformation of Homo Sapiens into Homo Ahimsa. Prayer, vision-holding and intention, inspired by unconditional love, are among our most powerful tools. Please feel free to use these prayers in your own meditations and to share them widely with others on social media, at places of worship, and in ceremonies. You are welcome to change the references to God and Divinity to align with what is most comfortable to you and your audience. *Please note the source of the prayer when you use it publicly.*

From Atonement to At-one-ment. Heavenly Love, You, who forgive all and love all, help us to make atonement to the animals of earth for atrocities performed by human beings against them for centuries. Link our spirits now with their spirits so that they may hear our cries of sorrow and shame for what our species has done to them. Dear brothers and sisters, we have tortured you, beaten, killed, sacrificed, skinned, dismembered, and eaten you. We have scorned you, laughed at your pain, taken your infants from you, chained you, caged you, forced you to carry our burdens, starved you, hooked you, stolen your feathers, and killed you without mercy. We have treated you like machines without feelings, ignoring your screams, but we were the machines without feelings, not you. You run from our knives, and we chase you as if we have the right to take your life so dear to you. We have taken advantage of your loyalty, even forced you to fight or run to the death for us, for a few dollars in our pockets. Century after century, you have given to us your friendship, fidelity, devotion, hard work, and you who live in the wild places, have given us glimpses of heaven in your beauty and looked at us with God's eyes. All the while, you have been crying out to us to wake up to our kinship with you.

But now we are awake and more are waking with us. Now we hear you. We go forward this day, bearing witness to our atrocities, bearing witness to your infinite gifts to us, and honoring your sacred nature. And here is our gift to you, and here is our atonement, that we will walk side by side with you, defending you, teaching people the truth about you, and working to bring an end to violence toward animals everywhere. We call upon the loving universe and the grace of God to help us as we humans join with all of you to affirm the advent of a new day in which our broken hearts are healed by your forgiveness, and your broken hearts are healed by our awakening to Truth; and to affirm the dawning of a new Heaven on Earth in which atonement becomes at-one-ment. *Peace to All Beings, p. 183.*

A prayer to say when you pass the meat, eggs, and dairy in the grocery store, restaurant, at a friend's home, etc.

"I see you, and I love you." That's it—simply—"I see you, and I love you." I wrote this prayer when someone asked me for a simple, easy-to-remember prayer to use when passing by the pieces of flesh, the gallons of baby cows' milk, the products made from it, and the eggs from tortured hens. To me, it means: I see who you really are. Even though I am looking at just a part of your body, I know you are pure spirit. In this moment, I see past the cruelty, the horror, the violence to *who you are* and have always been. The spirit in me greets the spirit in you. We are connected in love and gratitude. And I love you.

Meal Blessing

How blissful it is when our hearts awaken to the vast and mighty oceans of Universal Love. All life is sacred and interconnected. As we eat healing plants, we give thanks for our deep connection to the loving Earth and to all life. We give thanks that our bodies are holy temples and that we can nurture them with non-violent food filled with kindness and compassion.

The peace of doing no harm

We pray for help to bring us all to full awareness of who we can be as Homo Ahimsa and why we are here—to nurture, care for, and love ourselves and all beings. May every person find their own special path home to the truth. And in that home may we all feel the peace of doing no harm to animals or our own bodies. May all animals everywhere feel our love. May peace, compassion, love and respect prevail for all beings everywhere on earth.

Meals of kindness and compassion

We breathe in God's love and give thanks for the divine food meant for our human bodies. For it is plant food from the sacred Earth that nourishes and heals us. And it is by eating only plants that we do our part to end world hunger, environmental devastation, and animal suffering. May our meals every day help bring kindness and compassion to the world.

Envisioning a healed world

As our commitment to compassion grows and fills our hearts, help us to demonstrate to others what a beautiful world we can create together. May we look ahead and see what that beautiful, loving world looks like. We see fields and forests filled with animals who no longer fear us. Cows, horses, pigs, goats, chickens, and animals of the wilderness are caring for their families. Babies are running and jumping and playing with each other. Mothers and fathers are peacefully watching over their youngsters. The streams and rivers are clear and clean. The air is filled with the scent of sage and pine. The sky is a deep blue, and all that we see around us is healed and once again in balance. Our hearts fill with joy at the sight, and tears well up at the wonder of it all.

Love awakening
We live in harmony and mutual respect with all animals, all life. Divine kindness, compassion, love, and light express through us as we stand in awe and wonder to see this Loving Universe coming into being. May all animals and people and all of nature everywhere feel our love. May nurturing, gentle, tender, and yet powerful love awaken in all human hearts. May peace, compassion, love and respect prevail for the Earth, all animals and all people everywhere.

The unbroken roots of compassion
The roots of compassion, nonviolence and simple living run very deep and have been alive for thousands of years. These are our roots, and these values have come alive in us. We pray that they can awaken in everyone. We give thanks for all the many teachers who have kept this deep, abiding, unbroken source of kindness and compassion alive.

We are Love Walking; we are Love Being
We believe that whenever dogs wag their tails and kittens purr, more love fills the energy field of earth. We believe that every rainbow-hued bubble blown into the air by a delighted child does the same. We feel certain that every time our hearts expand with awe and wonder at the sight of a hummingbird, more love hovers into being. One tiny pebble landing in a pond creates perfect circles that radiate farther and farther out, vibrating beautiful designs far out beyond the first. Every ahimsa action we take fills the world with more love—love that cannot be lost. It is

constantly rippling out from us, radiating out from us wherever we are. We are Love Walking. We are Love Being.

Blessings of compassion

Divine Love, your will is compassion, joy, and freedom for all beings everywhere. We ask for the blessings of peace, compassion and freedom to go forth now to all the animals. We ask for the blessings of wisdom, enlightenment, and compassion to go forth now to all people who are in any way causing harm to animals. With joy and gratitude, we ask for the blessings of strength, grace and peace to go forth now to all people who are helping animals. May compassion prevail for all animals and all people everywhere.

Listening for Divine Ideas

We know the Truth that love overpowers violence and sets all beings free. We acknowledge the appearance of violence toward the animals of the world, and we let go of the misconception that this violence must continue. We know that violence has no power when faced with the unlimited power of God's Love. We give thanks that we all have the magnetic power to create, and we can choose to do our part to create a compassionate world. We give thanks that this universe is filled with limitless divine abundance and infinite compassion, not just for a few, but for all beings. We open our minds and hearts to the vast creative resources of the universe and listen for divine ideas to bring heaven to Earth.

Love never disappears

We have absolute faith that every big and little thing we do in love never disappears, but lasts forever. Cruelty and violence cannot survive in the world of love that we are creating day by day, prayer by prayer and action by action. The tipping point is near. As we continue to heal our sacred bodies with the rainbow colors of glorious plants, may we become messengers of divine mercy, compassion, and love wherever we go.

Vision of liberation

We give thanks for the divine awareness that we are part of a movement to change the world and bring peace at last to all beings. We ask for strength and wisdom to hold a vision of the beautiful new world that we are helping to create—a world in which slaughterhouses are being transformed into greenhouses; transport trucks are being transformed into sanctuary shelters; animal feed fields are rewilding into forests and meadows. We see *all people* around the world knowing deep in their hearts that animals are not ours to use or kill. And may the children of Earth walk confidently on the groundwork we have laid, to create with us a world of freedom and peace for all beings. We give thanks for this vision and ask for the inner peace and grace to bring it forth. We ask that the animals be filled with a deep knowing that true liberation is up ahead. May compassion and love reign over all the Earth for all beings. May nurturing, gentle, tender and, yet powerful, love awaken in all human hearts. May peace, compassion, love and respect prevail for all of nature and all earthlings everywhere.

The worldwide noon prayer

Compassion encircles the Earth for all beings everywhere.
Circleofcompassion.org

May all beings be happy.
May all beings be free.

NOTES

Introduction

1. McKosky, PJ, "No pasture here. Only pain," Poultry Press, Spring, 2019, Volume 28, Number 4.

2. Carman, Judy, *Peace to all beings*, Lantern Books, NY, p. 26.

3. Atkins, Emily: Why Animal Rights is the next frontier for the left, The New Republic, 3-14-19.

4. Quoted by Atkins, Emily: Why Animal Rights is the next frontier for the left, The New Republic, 3-14-19.

Chapter One

1. Ottesen, KK, Activist: Portraits of Courage, 2019, excerpt of interview of Jane Goodall, "Jane Goodall on Fighting Climate Change: 'The Window of Time is Closing.'" Quoted in the Washington Post, 12-3 19.

2. Rao, Sailesh, www.climatehealers.org.

3. Rao, Sailesh, www.climatehealers.org/animal-agriculture-white-paper.

4. "The 2018 Living Planet Report," zsl.org.

5. Vidal, John, "The rapid decline of the natural world is a crisis even bigger than climate change." Huffington Post, 3-15-19.

6. Ceballos, Gerardo; Ehrlich, Paul R.; Dirzo, Rodolfo; "Biological annihilation via the ongoing sixth mass extinction signaled by vertebrate population losses and declines," PNAS E6089-E6096; https://doi.org/10.1073/pnas. 1704949114, 7/25/17, 114 (30).

7. Bar-On, Yinon M.; Phillips, Rob; Milo, Ron; "The Biomass Distribution on Earth," Proceedings of the National Academy of Sciences of the U.S.A. 6-19-18.

8. "The Week," 5/10/19, p. 11, vol 19, issue 923, The Week.co.

9. Carrington, Damien, "IUCN red list reveals wildlife destruction from treetop to ocean floor," The Guardian, July 18, 2019.

10. Unifying Fields Foundation, "Beyond Climate Change: An integral solution." 5-1-19. White Paper, Unifyingfields.org.

11. Worldwatch Magazine, July, 2004, Worldwatch.org/node/549.

12. Poore, J and Nemecek, T. "Reducing Food's Environmental Impacts through Producers and Consumer," Science, 01 Jun 2018, Vol 360. Issue 6392, pp. 987-992.

13. Sanders, Bas, "Global Animal Slaughter Statistics and Charts," 10-10-18, www.Faunalytics.org.

14. www.awellfedworld.org.

15. Captain Paul Watson, "The Ocean is the Planet," Now You Know, 1-1-20, nowyouknow.ca/the-ocean-is-the-planet-capt-paul-watson.

16. Tuttle, Will, Ph. D. *World Peace Diet: Eating for Spiritual Health and Social Harmony*, 2005, 2016. Lantern Books, New York, NY, p. xx.

17. Volpe, Tina and Carman, Judy McCoy, *The Missing Peace*, Dreamriver Press, Flourtown, PA, 2009. Reprinted with a few edits.

18. Byrd, Jennifer, "Fair officials caution 4-H'ers to beware of shutterbugs: Board warns that animal rights activists may take photos to claim abuse," 7-29-04, Lawrence Journal World.

19. Blog post on Animal Place Sanctuary website, 7-24-17. http://animalplace.org/meet-fish/.

20. Neufeld, Franceen, Suffering Eyes: A Chronicle of Awakening, Purposeful Publishing House, Ontario, Canada, 2013.

21. "The Supreme Master Ching Hai News," No. 139, p. 39.

Chapter Two

1. Harari, Yuval Noah, *Homo Deus: A Brief History of Tomorrow*, Harper Collins, NY, NY, 2017.

2. Ibid.

3. Ibid.

4. Rao, Sailesh, "What is your menu choice?" www.climatehealers.org.

5. De Waal, Frans, *Mama's Last Hug: Animal emotions and what they tell us about ourselves*, 2019.

6. Carman, Judy, *Peace to All Beings: Veggie Soup for the Chicken's Soul*, Lantern Books, New York, NY 2003, p. 169.

Chapter Three

1. http://www.iawwai.com/NorthAmericanProphecies.html.

2. Macy, Joanna, www.AmazingMotherEarth.blogspot.com.

3. Love, Robert, quoting Camille Ameen, Woodstock attendee, in "Lives Touched by Woodstock, 50 Years On," in "AARP: The Magazine," August/September, 2019, p. 4.

4. Fry, Douglas, *Beyond War: The Human Potential for Peace*, Oxford University Press, 2007, p. 17.

5. Tuttle, Will, *The World Peace Diet,* p. 18.

6. Fillmore, Charles, "The Vegetarian," May 1920.

Chapter Four

1. Bosman, Julie, Taylor, Kate and Arango, Tim, New York Times: "A common trait among mass killers: Hatred Toward Women," August 10, 2019.

2. Kopf, Dan, "Why don't men volunteer as much as women," in online journal Priceonomics.com. December 17, 2015.

3. Fortune, Marie, "#MeToo Confronts the Patriarchy," "Reflections" magazine, Yale Divinity School, Fall, 2018

4. Ibid.

5. Will Tuttle, "Daily VegInspiration." Sign up at www.worldpeacediet.com.

6. Sri Mata Amritanandamayi Devi, "The Awakening of Universal Motherhood," An address given by Amma at the Global Peace Initiative of Women Religious and Spiritual Leaders, in Geneve, 10-7-02. Booklet published by Mata Amritanandamayi Mission Trust, Kerala, India, 2003.

7. Saunders, Carol, "Sacred Feminine Rising" www.TheSpiritualForum.org, August 25, 2019.

8. Amy Peck, "What is The Sacred Feminine," from the book, *Voices of the Sacred Feminine: Conversations to Reshape Our World*, Changemakers Books, 2014, Ed. By Rev. Dr. Karen Tate.

9. Eisler, Riane, *The Chalice and the Blade: Our History, Our Future*, Harper, San Francisco, CA, 1987.

Chapter Five

1. Vaclavik, Charles, *The Origin of Christianity: The Pacifism, Communalism and Vegetarianism of Primitive Christianity*, Kaweah Publishing Company, Platteville, WI, 1986, p. 401.

2. Akers, Keith, *The Lost Religion of Jesus: Simple Living and Nonviolence in Early Christianity*, Lantern Books, NY, NY, 2000, p. 3.

3. Ganesan, Rama, "Vegans Demanding Changes to Ancient Religions," online article, 11-18-15.

4. Father Donatello, email communication, 2019.

5. Johnson, Lisa. "The Religion of Ethical Veganism." *Journal of Animal Ethics*, vol. 5, no. 1, 2015, pp. 31–68.

6. McKenna, Paul. Reprinted with permission. Also included in the poster are Confucianism, Baha'i, Unitarianism, Native Spirituality, Taoism and Sikhism. Paul has had the poster translated into many different languages. Order the poster from: https://legacycafe.org/goldenrule.

7. Tuttle, Will, *The World Peace Diet*, p. 65.

8. Serkes, Sue, "Palestinians to protest Friday after Jews sacrifice lambs near Temple Mount," Times of Israel, 3-28-18. timesofisrael.com/palestinians-to-protest-Friday-after-jews-sacrifice-lambs-near-temple-mount.

9. Jacobs, Louis, *The Jewish Religion: A Companion*, 1st Edition, Oxford University Press: New York, p. 299, 1995. And Klein, Isaac, *A Guide to Jewish Religious Practice*, 1st Edition, Jewish Theological Seminary of America: New York, 1979, p. 208.

10. Carman, Judy, *Peace to All Beings: Veggie Soup for the Chicken's Soul*, Lantern Books, NY, NY 2003, p. 77.

11. Tuttle, Will, *The World Peace Diet*, p. 45.

12. Bekoff, Marc, "How to Apply the Golden Rule to Dogs and Other Nonhumans: This cross-species guideline is driven by data, decency, and heart." Psychology Today, 9/25/19.

13. Duse, Eleanora, "La Joie" magazine, Spring, 2013

Chapter Six

1. Harari, Yuval Noah, *Sapiens: A Brief History of Humankind*, Harper Collins, New York, 2015.

2. Stanescu, Vasile, "Fake News of Animal Advocacy: Response to the claim that only 2% (or less) of people in the United States are vegetarian," Guest Post on CriticalAnimal.com,7-1-2019. criticalanimal.com/2019/07/guest-post-response-to-claim-that-only.html

3. "The Future of Hamburgers," article in the magazine, "The Week: The Best of the U.S. and International Media", May 10, 2019, Vol 19, Issue 923, pp. 36-37.

4. Azhar, Azeem, "Reinventing Food, The Coming Disruption," notes by Diana Fox Carney. ExponentialView.co/p/-reinventing-food-the-coming-disruption.

5. Poore, J. and Nemecek, T., Science Magazine, "Reducing food's environmental impacts through producers and consumers," 1 June, 2018, Vol. 360, Issue 6392, pp 987-992; also on www.sciencemag.org.

6. "Mobile Veterinary Units," The David Sheldrick Wildlife Trust Newsletter, 2017, p. 40.

7. rancheradvocacy.org.

Chapter Seven

1. Rao, Sailesh, www.climatehealers.org.

POSTSCRIPT: April 25, 2020

As I was preparing this manuscript for publication, the COVID virus lockdown grabbed the world's attention. Theories and suspicions range widely about deaths, causes, cures, and government control. This is surely one of the strangest times any of us has ever known. But it is also one of the most hallowed and promising times for transformation that we have ever witnessed.

There have been many "pandemics." Most have been caused by the domestication, confinement and slaughter of animals; by nefarious experiments; by attacks on our immune systems; and ultimately by the law of cause and effect. The hell that is created for these innocent animals by human beings is beyond anyone's worst nightmare. We reap the consequences of confining them in filth where pathogens can grow out of control, making the animals sick, and then causing massive human disease. Current evidence is indicating that, just as there were no wars prior to animal agriculture, there may have been no pandemics either. The answer is right in front of us: no more animal agriculture means no more pandemics. With one simple change to eating only plants, we the people can save the world from future pandemics and all the lockdowns, death and suffering that they bring.

This is not the time to unite against another "enemy." It is time to unite, not *against* anything, but rather *for* our common dream to create a world of nonviolence, peace and freedom. Governments and corporations cannot solve the crises and are powerless to create a world of peace, because they are mired in the dying worldview of domination and violence and are motivated to act in ways that produce power and wealth for the elite, as well as tyranny over the people. So it is up to each of us. Everything we do and every prayer we pray now matters more than ever before.

The governments of the world are corrupt. The pharmaceutical industry reaps huge profits from pandemics and disease. We cannot rely on them. Homo Sapiens had the power to cause the pandemics; we, Homo Ahimsas, just as surely, have the power to stop them, while simultaneously creating a world in which our immune systems can flourish.

This is our window of opportunity, when the world is in this heightened state of fear, confusion, and uncertainty. Old ideas are shattering. This is humanity's chance to look beyond what we see with our eyes, beyond the follies and ignorance of Homo Sapiens. We are not victims of the dark forces of domination that have, up to now, caused endless death and destruction. Those forces have no power against the truth of Divine Love that lives in every single one of us and in all of nature and all beings if we will awaken to it and embrace it. We have to recognize that we are endowed with that Divine Love. We have to boldly claim our right to BE that. We are Homo Ahimsa rising. The time to take power and freedom back for all earthlings and heal ourselves and our world is urgently and obviously *now*. We can do this!

Peace to you and to all beings, Judy Carman